# Psychology
# of Aging

**Recent Titles in**
**Bibliographies and Indexes in Gerontology**

# *Psychology of Aging*

## An Annotated Bibliography

*Compiled by*
## Bert Hayslip, Jr.,
## Heather L. Servaty,
## and Amie S. Ward

**Bibliographies and Indexes in Gerontology, Number 28**
*Erdman B. Palmore, Series Adviser*

*Greenwood Press*
**Westport, Connecticut • London**

**Library of Congress Cataloging-in-Publication Data**

Hayslip, Bert.
Psychology of aging : an annotated bibliography / compiled by Bert
Hayslip, Jr., Heather L. Servaty, and Amie S. Ward.
p.     cm.—(Bibliographies and indexes in gerontology, ISSN
0743–7560; no. 28)
Includes bibliographical references and indexes.
ISBN 0–313–29376–7 (alk. paper)
1. Aging—Psychological aspects—Bibliography.   2. Aged—
Psychology—Bibliography.   I. Servaty, Heather L.   II. Ward, Amie
S.   III. Title.   IV. Series.
Z7204.A42H392   1995
[BF724.8] . H392 1995
016.15567—dc20        95–6291

British Library Cataloguing in Publication Data is available.

Library of Congress Catalog Card Number: 95–6291
ISBN: 0–313–29376–7
ISSN: 0743–7560

First published in 1995

Greenwood Press, 88 Post Road West, Westport, CT 06881
An imprint of Greenwood Publishing Group, Inc.

Printed in the United States of America

∞™

The paper used in this book complies with the
Permanent Paper Standard issued by the National
Information Standards Organization (Z39.48–1984).

10 9 8 7 6 5 4 3 2

*Special thanks are extended to Lee Ward for
her enthusiasm and skill in typing, editing, and
in the formatting of the manuscript.*

# Contents

# Series Foreword

The annotated bibliographies in this series provide answers to the fundamental question, "What is known?" Their purpose is simple, yet profound: to provide comprehensive reviews and references for the work done in various fields of gerontology. They are based on the fact that it is no longer possible for anyone to comprehend the vast body of research and writing in even one sub-specialty without years of work.

This fact has become true only in recent years. When I was an undergraduate (Class of '52) I think no one at Duke had even heard of gerontology. Almost no one in the world was identified as a gerontologist. Now there are over 6,000 professional members of the Gerontological Society of America. When I was an undergraduate there were no courses in gerontology. When I was an undergraduate there was only one gerontological journal (the *Journal of Gerontology*, begun in 1945). Now there are over forty professional journals and several dozen books in gerontology published each year.

The reasons for this dramatic growth are well known: the dramatic increase in numbers of aged, the shift from family to public responsibility for the security and care of the elderly, the recognition of aging as a "social problem," and the growth of science in general. It is less well known that this explosive growth in knowledge has developed the need for new solutions to the old problem of comprehending and "keeping up" with a field of knowledge. The old indexes and library card catalogues have become increasingly inadequate for the job. On-line computer indexes and abstracts are one solution but make no evaluative selections nor organize sources logically as is done here. These annotated bibliographies are also more widely available than on-line computer indexes.

These bibliographies will obviously be useful for students, teachers, and researchers who need to know what research has (or has not) been done in their field. This particular bibliography will also be useful to mental health workers, psychologists, and other professionals working with elders. The annotations usually contain enough information so that the user does not have to search out the original articles.

In the past, the "review of literature" has often been haphazard and was rarely comprehensive, because of the large investment of time (and money) that would be required by a truly comprehensive review. Now, using these bibliographies, researchers and others concerned with this topic can be more confident that they are not missing important previous research and other reports; they can be more confident that they are not duplicating past efforts and "reinventing the wheel." It may well become standard and expected practice for researchers to consult such bibliographies, even before they start their research.

The research and writing relevant to the psychology of older persons has become a large and rapidly growing field, especially in the last few decades. This is attested to by the 546 references in this bibliography, and by the wide variety of disciplines represented here.

The authors have done an outstanding job of covering the recent literature and organizing it into easily accessible form. Not only are the entries organized into 14 chapters (in alphabetical order within each chapter), but there is a preface, and a comprehensive subject index and author index.

Thus one can look for relevant material in this volume in several ways: (1) look up a given subject in the subject index; (2) look up a given author in the author index; or (3) turn to the chapter that covers the subject in which you are interested.

Professor Hayslip is exceptionally well-qualified to produce this bibliography. He has long been a specialist in this area, has done significant research, and published numerous relevant articles.

So it is with great pleasure that we add this bibliography to our series. We believe you will find this volume to be the most useful, comprehensive, and easily accessible reference work in its field. I will appreciate any comments you care to send me.

Erdman B. Palmore
Center for the Study of Aging and Human Development
Box 3003, Duke University Medical Center
Durham, NC 27710

# *Preface*

This annotated bibliography covers a variety of content areas, reflecting research in the psychological processes of aging. We utilized several criteria for an entry's inclusion: currency, representativeness and historical significance. To this end, journal articles, books, and book chapters have been included. We feel that this diverse collection of entries will provide the reader with a sampling of lines of research, investigators, and reviews of the literature so that critical issues in psychogerontology can be understood. Consequently, this bibliography should be most helpful to both graduate students and beginning researchers as well as to gerontological practitioners.

For the most part, we have concentrated on sources that span the last 10-15 years, with occasional entries that are more dated. Some of these latter sources might be considered "classics" in the field, of which we feel no student should be unaware. We made no attempt to sample equally from each interest area; it is clear that aging research is growing at a greater rate in some domains than in others. Consequently, more entries reflect current work in, for example, cognitive aging than in the psychological aspects of work and retirement.

As space was limited, we have tried to select sources whose coverage was representative of work in the area, though there are obviously many others that could have been included, depending on other considerations such as redundancy or specificity of coverage.

In light of our goal to provide a useful guide to research in the psychology of aging, both authored and edited books as well as book chapters have been given substantial weight as they are more likely to represent integrated summaries of research, each with its own list of primary references. In addition, journal articles that are, for the most part, no more than 10 years old, and in most cases, those that are much more recent, have been emphasized as well. These draw on scientific outlets in the field such as <u>Psychology and Aging</u>, <u>The Journal of Gerontology</u>, <u>The Gerontologist</u>, <u>Experimental Aging Research</u>, <u>International Journal of Aging and Human Development</u>, and <u>Developmental Psychology</u>. While many of these sources focus specifically on older adults, other are age comparative in nature, based on our belief that psychological aging is best viewed in the context of the life span frame of reference. For the most part, textbooks have been avoided in place of other more substantive references.

Entries in this bibliography have been organized into several areas of focus: theory, research methods, psychophysiology, sensory-perceptual processes, learning and memory, intelligence, creativity, personality, interpersonal relationships, assessment, mental health and psychopathology, therapy and intervention, work and retirement, and death and dying. In each case, comments on a source's content, or in the case of journal articles, some statement regarding a study's purposes and findings has been made. For most authored and edited books, some indication of each chapter's content has been provided. As a general rule, while an entry will be unique to an area, there are purposeful duplications where a source cuts across several areas of focus, as might be true for an edited book.

While there is no substitute for a thorough literature search, we hope that the reader will find this annotated bibliography useful as a guide to recent research and integrative reviews of the literature in the psychology of aging.

BHJ
HLS
ASW
September, 1994

# *Psychology of Aging*

# 1

# *Theory in the Psychology of Aging*

T1    Baltes, P.B. (1987). Theoretical propositions of life span developmental psychology: On the dynamics between growth and decline. Developmental Psychology, 23, 611-626.
        Excellent overview of the principles of development from a lifespan perspective.

T2    Baltes, P.B., & Baltes, M.M. (1990). Psychological perspectives on successful aging: The model of selective optimization with compensation. In P.B. Baltes & M.M. Baltes (Eds.), Successful aging: Perspectives from the behavioral sciences (pp. 1-34). Cambridge: Cambridge University Press.
        Outlines research in the psychology of aging in terms of seven propositions and presents one model of successful aging in view of these propositions. Emphasis on selective optimization and compensation as processes which allow older persons to adapt to changed life circumstances.

T3    Baltes, P.B., Cornelius, S. W., & Nesselroade, J.R. (1979). Cohort effects in developmental psychology. In J. Nesselroade & P. Baltes (Eds.), Longitudinal research in the study of behavior and development (pp. 61-87). New York: Academic Press.
        Selective review of research on cohort effects in developmental psychology, with implications for both theory and research.

T4    Baltes, P.B., & Danish, S.J. (1980). Intervention in life-span development and aging: Issues and concepts. In R. Turner and H.

Reese (Eds.), Life-span developmental psychology: Intervention (pp. 49-75). New York: Academic Press.

Examines the definitions of and assumptions about intervention, emphasizing plasticity of behavior, differential aging and the generation and application of knowledge about development as organizing themes.

T5    Birren, J.E., & Birren, B.A. (1990). Theory and measurement in the psychology of aging. In J.E. Birren & K.W. Schaie (Eds.), Handbook of the psychology of aging (pp. 3-20). New York: Academic Press.

Excellent overview of theory in a historical context. Discussion of metamodels in the psychology of aging as well as the concept of development is well done.

T6    Birren, J. E., & Schaie, K. W. (1985). Handbook of the psychology of aging. New York: Van Nostrand Reinhold.

Although dated, the second edition of this seminal text contains excellent chapters on such topics as theory, research methods, measurement, social influences on behavior, cognition, affect, health, genetic and neural aspects of aging behavior, personality, and clinical gerontology.

T7    Brim, O.G., & Phillips, D.A. (1988). The life-span intervention cube. In E.M. Hetherington, R.M. Lerner, & P.B. Baltes (Eds.), Child development in life-span perspective (pp. 270-300). Hillsdale, NJ: Lawrence Erlbaum.

Thought provoking discussion of the rationale and design of intervention across the lifespan emphasizing specificity of interventions and their contextual value.

T8    Bronfenbrenner, U. (1977). Toward an experimental ecology of human development. American Psychologist, 32, 513-531.

Seminal paper looking at the dynamics of the changing person and a changing environment from a systems perspective.

T9    Danish, S. (1981). Life-span development and intervention: A necessary link. Counseling Psychologist, 9, 40-43.

Ties together assumptions about development from a life span perspective and principles of intervention from a systems perspective.

T10   Danish, S. J., Smyer, M.A., & Nowak, C.A. (1980). Developmental intervention: Enhancing life-event processes. In P. Baltes & O. Brim (Eds.), Life-span development and behavior: V. 3 (pp. 339-366). New York: Academic Press.

Defines the construct of intervention in the context of the many dimensions of life events. Uses retirement to discuss the functions that intervention might play.

T11     Dannefer, D. (1992). On the conceptualization of context in developmental discourse: Four meanings of context and their implication. In D. L. Featherman, R. L. Lerner & M. Perlmutter (Eds.), <u>Lifespandevelopment and behavior: V.11</u> (pp. 84-111). Hillsdale, NJ: Lawrence Erlbaum.
        Theoretical account of the many meanings that context can have as a determinant of developmental change. Gives specific and critical attention to the issue of contextual influences on adult developmental change. Diversity among aged persons is understood via a variety of views about the importance of context in adult development.

T12     Dannefer, D., & Perlmutter, M. (1990). Development as a multidimensional process: Individual and social constituents. <u>Human Development</u>, <u>33</u>, 108-137.
        Gives special attention to the explication of social and environmental influences on psychological development and identifies several developmental and social processes which might help to expand knowledge about the process by which adults dynamically interact with their environments.

T13     Demick, J. (1994). The parameters of adult development. <u>Journal of Adult Development</u>, <u>1</u>, 1-5.
        Attempts to define critical questions and/or dimensions that might guide theory and research in adult development, emphasizing, for example, multi-leveled development, transdisciplinary collaboration and the ongoing relationship between theory and research.

T14     Dowd, J.J. (1990). Ever since Durkheim: The socialization of human development. <u>Human Development</u>, <u>33</u>, 138-159.
        Using Riegel's dialectics as a base, critically examines development across the lifespan from within the structure of human society, emphasizing the mutual influence of adults and society on one another.

T15     Eisdorfer, C. (1983). Conceptual models of aging: Challenge of a new frontier. <u>American Psychologist</u>, <u>38</u>, 197-202.
        Explores new ways of defining the process of aging and expectations one has of older adults and their implications for mental health.

T16     Eisdorfer, C., & Lawton, M. P. (1973). <u>Psychology of adult development and aging</u>. Washington, DC: American Psychological Association.
         Groundbreaking edited volume containing chapters on cognition, personality, attitudes toward aging, person-environment relations, psychophysiology, and a variety of clinically-oriented chapters.

T17     Haraven, T. (1986). Historical changes in the social construction of the life course. <u>Human Development</u>, <u>29</u>, 171-180.
         Examines the emergence of late adulthood in light of the familial, social and economic conditions to which they must adapt. Emphasizes the historical context in which aging takes place.

T18     Hayslip, B., & Panek, P. (1993). <u>Adult development and aging</u>. New York: Harper Collins.
         Topical examination of a variety of theoretical and empirical issues in adulthood. Takes a lifespan approach to the study of later life, emphasizing the many dimensions of change in behavior across time.

T19     Hetherington, E.M., & Baltes, P.B. (1988). Child psychology and lifespan development. In R. Lerner & M. Perlmutter (Eds.), <u>Child development in life-span perspective</u> (pp. 1-19). Hillsdale, NJ: Lawrence Erlbaum.
         Examines child development from a lifespan perspective, integrating what is known about the similarities and differences between children and adults.

T20     Hudson, F. M. (1991). <u>The adult years: Mastering the art of self-renewal</u>. San Francisco: Jossey-Bass.
         Interesting nonscientific book exploring the challenges to personal growth and development in the adult years. Includes specific discussions of late adulthood. Incorporates historical change as a dimension which must be accounted for in our continued push toward positive self-growth.

T21     Hultsch, D.F., & Hickey, T. (1978). External validity in the study of human development: Theoretical and methodological issues. <u>Human Development</u>, <u>21</u>, 76-91.
         Examines the construct of external validity from numerous theoretical perspectives, emphasizing the comparison of mechanism and dialectics.

T22     Kausler, D. F. (1991). Methodological issues, explanation, and theory in experimental aging research. In D. F. Kausler (Ed.), <u>Experimental</u>

psychology, cognition, and human aging (pp. 1-70). New York: Springer-Verlag.

Outstanding high level discussion of theory and research methods in the psychology of aging. Extremely well documented and comprehensive in its presentation.

T23    Kimmel, D. C., & Moody, H. R. (1990). Ethical issues in gerontological research and services. Handbook of the psychology of aging (pp. 490-502). New York: Academic Press.

Written for those new to the field, this chapter explores ethical considerations in the design and implementation of research with older persons as well as the delivery of psychological services to elderly adults.

T24    Lerner, R. M. (1984). On the nature of human plasticity. Cambridge: Cambridge University Press.

Multidisciplinary approach to plasticity of development across the lifespan. Excellent, thought provoking approach to the potential for human behavioral change.

T25    Lerner, R.M. (1985). Individual and context in developmental psychology: Conceptual and theoretical issues. In J.R. Nesselroade & A. Von Eye (Eds.), Individual development and social change (pp. 155-188). New York: Academic Press.

Explores the advantages and disadvantages of a "person-in-context" model of development, looking at this approach to development and aging from a variety of perspectives.

T26    Lerner, R.M. (1986). Concepts and theories of human development. Reading, MA: Addison-Wesley.

Readable and well-written examination of major approaches to human development. Suitable for beginning level graduate or upper level undergraduates.

T27    Levinson, D. (1986). A conception of adult development. American Psychologist, 41, 3-13.

Succinctly describes Levinson's construct of the life structure and its changes over time for males. Exemplifies a stage approach to adult development and aging.

T28    Montada, L., & Schmitt, M. (1982). Issues in applied developmental psychology: A life-span perspective. In P. B. Baltes & O. G. Brim, Jr., (Eds.), Life-span development and behavior: V. 4 (pp. 2-34). New York: Academic Press.

This well written chapter defines applied developmental psychology and its goals as well as advocating a scientific basis for practitioner-based decisions and interventions.

T29     Morse, C. K. (1993). Does variability increase with age? An archival study of cognitive measures. Psychology and Aging, 8, 156-164.
        Based on a five year examination of studies, the authors found that variability was greater for measures of reaction time, memory, and fluid intelligence. Important to the extent that generalizations about older persons' performance may be limited.

T30     Nelson, A.E., & Dannefer, D. (1992). Aged heterogeneity: Fact or fiction? The fate of diversity in gerontological research. The Gerontologist, 32, 17-23.
        Reviews the evidence for increased individual differences in the aging process utilizing existing research as a means for to exploring this construct.

T31     Oerter, R. (1986). Developmental tasks through the life-span: A new approach to an old concept. In P. B. Baltes, D. L. Featherman & R. M. Lerner (Eds.), Life-span development and behavior: V. 7 (pp. 233-271). Hillsdale, NJ: Lawrence Erlbaum.
        Reviews the construct of developmental tasks, suggesting that they be redefined so to reflect historical change and to be more dynamic in nature.

T32     Palmore, E. B. (1984). Handbook on the aged in the United States. Westport, CT: Greenwood Press.
        A comprehensive, though now dated, examination of many aspects of aging and older adults. It includes specific edited chapters on such topics as ethnicity, suicide, homosexuality, crime, addiction, centenarians, retirement, and widowhood. Extremely well-referenced.

T33     Palmore, E. B. (1970). Normal aging. Reports from the Duke longitudinal study, 1955-1969. Durham, NC: Duke University Press.
        Detailed presentation of the longitudinal findings from the Duke University study. This monograph summarizes and integrates findings on the psychosocial aspects of aging. Very technical scientific papers are reprinted in their entirety.

T34     Palmore, E. B. (1974). Normal aging II: Reports from the Duke longitudinal studies: 1970-1973. Durham, NC: Duke University Press.
        This second volume in the series builds upon and extends those findings presented earlier. Equally, comprehensive in scope, it

encompasses new longitudinal data of a psychosocial nature that is both conceptually and methodologically rich.

T35    Palmore, E. B. (1985). Normal aging III: Reports from the Duke longitudinal studies: 1975-1984. Durham, NC: Duke University Press.
Presents a more detailed analysis of the data gathered in each of the two Duke longitudinal studies. Chapters are organized into four areas: physical aging, mental health/mental illness, psychological aging, and social aging. Emphasizes the interdisciplinary nature of aging research that yields valuable data regarding age changes along a number of dimensions.

T36    Poon, L. W. (1980). Aging in the 1980's: Psychological issues. Washington, DC: American Psychological Association.
Excellent edited volume containing chapters dealing with theory, research methods, measurement, cognition, stress and coping, psychophysiology, psychopharmacology, and relationships.

T37    Reese, H. (1994). The data/theory dialectic; The nature of scientific progress. In S. Cohen & H. Reese (Eds.), Life-span developmental psychology: Methodological contributions (pp. 1-27). Hillsdale, NJ: Lawrence Erlbaum.
Explores the ongoing dynamic relationship between data and theory.

T38    Reese, H., & Smyer, M. (1983). The dimensionalization of life events. In E.J. Callahan & K.A. McCluskey (Eds.), Life span developmental psychology: Nonnormative life events (pp. 1-34). New York: Academic Press.
Proposes a novel, if not highly complex, approach to the understanding and categorization of life events emphasizing several aspects of each such as their context, self-other focus, degree of impact and nature of control by persons who are experiencing them.

T39    Riegel, K. F. (1976). The dialectics of human development. American Psychologist, 31, 689-700.
Examines human development from a dialectical perspective. Excellent overview of this approach to development.

T40    Riley, M.W. (1986). The dynamism of life stages: Roles, people, and age. Human Development, 29, 150-156.
Explores the basis for life stages: Their development, definition and meaning for persons. Emphasis on the relativeness of this construct, using retirement and family life as examples.

T41      Rosow, I. (1978). What is a cohort and why? Human Development,
         21, 66-75.
         Explores the conceptual and definitional problems associated with
         cohort effects in adult development and aging.

T42      Schaie, K. W. (1991). Annual review of gerontology and geriatrics V.
         11. New York: Springer.
         Covers a wide variety of topics on the psychology of aging and
         includes chapters on memory, learning, intelligence, self concept, well-
         being, emotion, social relationships, exercise, aging and work,
         depression, caregiving, and adjustment to institutionalization. Excellent
         reviews of research.

T43      Schick, F. L. & Schick, R. (1994). Statistical handbook on aging
         Americans. Phoenix, AZ: Oryx Press.
         Excellent statistical resource for information relevant to psycholo-
         gists based on 1990 census data. Includes up-to-date data on education,
         elder abuse and health.

T44      Schroots, J.J., & Birren, J.E. (1990). Concepts of time and aging in
         science. In J.E. Birren & K. W. Schaie (Eds.), Handbook of the
         psychology of aging (pp. 45-64). New York: Academic Press.
         Explores the diverse meanings of time as a marker of the aging
         process from a variety of perspectives.

T45      Steenbarger, B.N. (1991). All the world is not a stage: Emerging
         contextualist themes in counseling and development. Journal of
         Counseling and Development, 70, 288-296.
         Excellent application of the principles of life span developmental
         psychology to counseling research and practice. Discusses the
         shortcomings of classical stage-based theories of human development
         when extended to counseling applications. Suggests that counselors are
         turning to contextual models of development that emphasize process
         over outcome. Reviews key assumptions of contextualism, as embodied
         in social role theory and the life-span developmental tradition,
         highlighting relevant theory and research. Ends with specific implicat-
         ions of contextualism for future counseling research and practice.

T46      Stewart, R. (1994). Reflections on a model approach to metapsych-
         ology. In S. Cohen & H. Reese (Eds.), Life-span developmental
         psychology: Methodological implications (pp. 1-28). Hillsdale, NJ:
         Lawrence Erlbaum.

Examines the question of the inherent incomparability of models of development, with specific concern for the organismic vs. mechanistic models of adult development and aging.

T47    Storandt, M., & VanderBos, G. R. (1990). The adult years: Continuity and change. Washington, DC: American Psychological Association.
This text contains APA Master Lectures examining personality, cognitive, health, clinical and policy-related aspects of adult development and aging.

T48    Thompson, R. (1988). Early development in life span perspective. In P. Baltes, D. Featherman, & R. Lerner (Eds.), Life span development and behavior, V, 9 (130-172). Hillsdale, NJ: Lawrence Erlbaum.
Discusses the intersection of child development and life span development in the context of several issues such as plasticity and multi-dimensionality. Addresses the extent to which the two perspectives regarding development are necessary.

T49    Viney, L.L. (1992). Can we see ourselves changing? Toward a personal construct model of adult development. Human Development, 35, 65-75.
Approaches adult development from a constructivist perspective, with implications for theory development and research.

T50    Wohlwill, J. F. (1970). The age variable in psychological research. Psychological Review, 77, 49-64.
Classic paper examining the conceptual status of chronological age in the design and implementation of research in the psychology of aging. Contrasts views about age as an independent versus dependent variable in developmental research.

T51    Wohlwill, J.F. (1973). The study of behavioral development. New York: Academic Press.
This classic thoroughly examines several important theoretical and methodological issues in development which are equally important in the study of children and older adults.

# 2

# *Research Methodology*

R1 Baltes, P. B. (1968). Longitudinal and cross-sectional sequences in the study of age and generation effects. <u>Human Development</u>, <u>11</u>, 145-171.

 Classic paper discussing internal and external validity issues in traditional developmental designs as well as the author's bifactorial model of data collection.

R2 Baltes, P. B. (1987). Theoretical propositions of life-span developmental psychology: On the dynamics between growth and decline. <u>Developmental Psychology</u>, <u>23</u>, 611-626.

 One of the fields foremost theorists in lifespan developmental psychology discusses his approach to developmental research in a conceptual yet applicable framework. Although the paper is largely theoretical, the author discusses testing-the-limits as a practical research method to study variability in older adults. Outlines many important factors that should be considered by all researchers in the field in a readable, organized format.

R3 Baltes, P. B., Reese, H. W., & Nesselroade, J. R. (1988). <u>Life-span developmental psychology: Introduction to research methods</u>. Monterey, CA: Brooks-Cole.

 Excellent overview of the conceptual and especially the methodological aspects of developmental research. Readable interpretation of highly complex methodological issues.

R4 Birren, J. E., & Renner, J. V. (1977). Research on the psychology of aging: Principles and experimentation. In J. E. Birren & K. W. Schaie

(Eds.), Handbook of the psychology of aging (pp. 3-38). New York: Van Nostrand Reinhold.

Excellent, though now somewhat dated discussion of research and theory in the psychology of aging. Good coverage of experimental gerontology.

R5      Hertzog, C. (1987). Applications of structural equation models in gerontological research. In K. W. Schaie (Ed.), Annual review of gerontology and geriatrics: V. 7 (pp. 265-294). New York: Springer.

Relatively nontechnical discussion of both measurement and structural regression components of structural equation model in gerontological research. The foci in this context are on information processing and intelligence.

R6      Hertzog, C. (1990). On the utility of structural equation models for developmental research. In P. B. Baltes, D. L. Featherman & R. L. Lerner (Eds.), Life-span development and behavior: V 10 (pp. 257-290).

Explores misconceptions about the use of structural equation modeling (SEM) in developmental research and discusses the proper use of SEM in longitudinal designs.

R7      Hoyer, W. J., Raskind, C., & Abrahams, J. (1984). Research practices in the psychology of aging: A survey of research. Journal of Gerontology, 39, 44-48.

Reviews current state of aging research methods, noting problems in sampling and methods of subject recruitment as well as pointing out the continued popularity of cross-sectional designs.

R8      Hultsch, D. F., & Deutsch, F. (1981). Adult development and aging: A lifespan perspective. New York: McGraw-Hill.

Specific chapters discuss the ethical issues involved in aging research, including informed consent, subjects knowledge about the true nature of the research, misinformation, coercing subjects to participate in research, failure to honor promises and commitments, exposing subjects to physical or mental stress, invasion of privacy, failure to maintain confidentiality, and withholding benefits from participants.

R9      Kunkel, M. A., & Williams, C. (1991). Age and expectations about counseling: Two methodological perspectives. Journal of Counseling and Development, 70, 314-320.

Contrasts quantitative self-report with phenomenological methods of data collection in studying age differences in expectations about counseling.

R10     Kausler, D. H. (1991). <u>Experimental psychology, cognition, and</u>
        <u>human aging, second edition</u>. New York: Springer-Verlag.
        This excellent text focuses on research methodology in traditional
        areas of experimental aging research. Contains in-depth descriptions
        of cross-sectional, longitudinal and sequential designs. Discusses the
        identification of age-sensitive and age-insensitive processes, alternatives
        to traditional interaction research, and theoretical perspectives of
        research methodolgy in aging research. Traditionally studied areas of
        experimental psychology, such as sensation and perception, memory,
        learning, and intelligence are thoroughly addressed in a methodological
        context.

R11     Nelson, E. A., & Dannefer, D. (1992). Aged heterogeneity: Fact or
        fiction? The fate of diversity in gerontological research. <u>The</u>
        <u>Gerontologist</u>, <u>32</u>, 17-23.
        A meta-analytic investigation of 185 longitudinal and cross-sectional
        studies critically examining the use of variability measures and other
        measures of individual differences in the gerontological literature.
        Reports that means and averages are over-represented, especially in
        longitudinal studies, even though closer examination of the data from
        these studies revealed increasing variability with age. Suggests that
        heterogeneity is often overlooked in gerontological research.

R12     Raykov, D., Tomer, A., & Nesselroade, J. (1991). Reporting
        structural equation modeling results in Psychology and Aging: Some
        proposed quidelines. <u>Psychology and Aging</u>, <u>6</u>, 499-503.
        Discusses the many computer programs available to do SEM with
        recommendations regarding criteria for reporting findings that would
        allow for more objective evaluation and comparison of data.

R13     Rosow, I. (1978). What is a cohort and why? <u>Human Development</u>,
        <u>21</u>, 65-75.
        This paper is quite theoretical as well as methodological in its
        perspective on using cohorts as a means of assigning subjects.
        Discusses the problems in research that have developed due to the
        inappropriate use of subjects grouped on factors other than cohort, and
        describes the necessary conditions by which cohorts are defined. Uses
        classic theoretical models as examples to discuss the applications of
        cohort and identifies relevant problems, such as cohort boundaries,
        distinctive cohort experiences, and differential cohort effects. Also
        discusses limits of the use of cohorts.

R14    Russell, D. W., & Duckwalter, K. C. (1992). Researching and
       evaluating model geriatric mental health programs: III. Statistical
       analysis issues. Archives of Psychiatric Nursing, 8, 151-162.
           Discusses methods of evaluating mental health programs for older
       adults, focusing on choosing appropriate statistical tests and analyzing
       data from experimental and randomized designs. Also discusses quasi-
       experimental designs in which pre-existing groups of older adults are
       assigned to conditions, non-equivalent samples, and sophisticated tech-
       niques, such as analysis of covariance and interrupted time-series
       analysis.

R15    Salthouse, T. A., & Kausler, D. H. (1985) Memory methodology in
       maturity. In C. J. Brainerd & M. Pressley (Eds.), Basic processes in
       memory development: Progress in cognitive development research.
       New York: Springer-Verlag.
           Discusses methods to maximize distinguishability between contrasted
       groups, and the problems inherent in certain designs. In particular,
       caution in interpreting interaction effects is advised, due to ceiling or
       floor effects that are common in this area of research. The authors
       urge the use of tasks that are neither too easy nor too difficult to
       maximize divergence between groups. They also warn against
       performing transformations and other manipulations on nonlinear data,
       since nonlineartiy is often a valid pattern of results in aging research.

R16    Schaie, K. W. (1965). A general model for the study of developmen-
       tal problems. Psychological Bulletin, 64, 92-107.
           This classic methods paper describes sequential designs and forms
       the basis for Schaies trifactorial Model. Discusses potential confounds
       in developmental research in the context of widely used designs, such
       as longitudinal and cross-sectional and describes sophisticated design
       techniques to control for each of these confounds. Designs are
       discussed in terms of the variables of interest to the researcher, and are
       presented logically, though the material is difficult.

R17    Schaie, K. W. (1984). Historical time and cohort effects. In K.
       McCluskey & H. Reese (Eds.), Life-span developmental psychology:
       Historical and generation effects (pp. 1-16). New York: Academic
       Press.
           Readable account of the author's revisions in how cohort and age
       can be disentangled from calendar time in the context of assessing
       sources of developmental change.

R18     Schaie, K. W. (1986). Beyond calendar definitions of age, time, and cohort: The general developmental model revisted. Developmental Review, 6, 252-277.

        This empirically based article examines Schaie's newer ideas about the trifactorial model's components and their implications for developmental design. Requires some familiarity with Schaie's previous work.

R19     Schaie, K. W. (1992). The impact of methodological changes in gerontology. International Journal of Aging and Human Development, 35, 19-29.

        Readable yet inclusive discussion of the development of more sophisticated research designs in aging and their impact on the quality of knowledge about the aging process.

R20     Schaie, K. W. (1993). Ageist language in psychological research. American Psychologist, 48, 49-51.

        Discusses the potential problems of ageist language in empirical research and provides recommendations for the use of alternative language. Although many of the recommendations are applicable to language used when discussing age in any context, focuses on the use of alternative language in the description of research topics, study designs, methodology and subjects used, and analysis and interpretation of results.

R21     Schaie, K. W., & Baltes, P. B. (1975). On sequential designs in developmental research: Description or explanation? Human Development, 18, 384-390.

        Attempts to resolve different points of view regarding the adequacy of sequential designs in assessing developmental change. Requires familiarity with the developmental designs advocated by each author.

R22     Sinnott, J., Harris, C., Block, M., Collesano, S., & Jacobsen, S. (1985). Applied research in aging. Boston: Little-Brown.

        Well done presentation of a variety of applied topics and issues in gerontological research. Ethics of research section is unique.

R23     Smolak, L. (1993). Adult development. Englewood Cliffs, NJ: Prentice Hall.

        This general text offers a life-span development perspective on changes that occur throughout adulthood. Although the book is quite comprehensive in the areas of physiological, social, emotional, intellectual, and motivational change, it also provides an in-depth description of research methodology in the study of adult development. Particular emphasis is placed on types of validity, statistical evidence, and ethics in research, as well as typical models of adult development and the goals of life-span developmental research.

R24     Storandt, M., & Hudson, W. (1975). Misuse of the analysis of covariance in aging research and some partial solutions. Experimental Aging Research, 1, 121-125.

Discusses the problems inherent in using analysis of covariance in explanatory research, such as nonorthogonality and inequality on most independent variables when comparing younger and older persons. Suggests using regression analysis as an alternative to analysis of covariance.

R25     Thomas, J. L. (1992). Adulthood and aging. Boston: Allyn & Bacon.

This broad-based text examines change throughout early, middle, and later life with a multicultural life-span developmental perspective. A large portion of the book is devoted to encouraging the reader to take a more critical view of research in the area. In this context, the author provides an overview of classical and contemporary research and theory, and discusses issues such as sampling, measurement, and analysis and how these variables can affect outcome. An appendix points to statistical tools commonly used in developmental research.

R26     Woodruff-Pak, D. S. (1988). Psychology and aging. Englewood Cliffs, NJ: Prentice Hall.

This text provides a general overview of many methods used in the study of aging. Chapter 2 is particularly devoted to the subject, but the remainder of the book offers excellent descriptions and references to literature dealing with research methodology in the field. The methods chapter emphasizes the scientific method in general, classical designs, explanatory analytical developmental research, and ethics.

# 3

# *Psychophysiology*

PH1    Birren, J. E. (1960). Behavioral theories of aging. In N. W. Shock (Ed.), Aging -- Some social and biological aspects. Washington, DC: American Association for the Advancement of Science.

     This chapter was the first to describe the underarousal theory of aging. Explains that the observed psychomotor slowing of older adults may be due to reduced physiological activation. This reduced activation leads to lowered drives and motivation, which leads to less interaction with the environment. As a result, the older adult has less opportunity to engage in psychological processes, such as perception, acquisition, manipulation of symbols, and storage. Support for this hypothesis is provided by EEG studies which describe the slowing of the alpha rhythm with age.

PH2    Bondareff, W. (1980). Compensatory loss of axosomatic synapses in the dentate gyrus of the senescent rat. Mechanisms of Aging and Development, 12, 221-229.

     Describes a model of aging based on observations of "compensatory" losses of excitatory and inhibitory synapses. Suggests that the lower autonomic responsiveness observed in older adults is a result of neuronal degradation of the reticular formation. Inhibitory influences by the anterior cortex is therefore lessened, and frontal functions are thus less efficient.

PH3    Carskadon, M. A. (1982). Sleep fragmentation, sleep loss, and sleep need in the elderly. Gerontologist, 22.

     Used a five-night sleep deprivation and recovery paradigm to examine sleep patterns in subjects aged 61-77 years. One night of sleep deprivation resulted in subjects spending more time in stages III and IV and significantly less in stage I than control. Subjects also had fewer wakenings for two nights following sleep deprivation. Suggests that older persons should spend only six hours per night in bed in order to improve the quantity of time spent in deep sleep and the quality of sleep overall.

PH4     Coleman, R. M., Miles, L. E., Guilleminault, C. C., Zarcone, V. P., Van Den Hoed, J., & Dement, W. C. (1981). Sleep-wake disorders in the elderly: A polysomnographic analysis. Journal of the American Geriatrics Society, 29, 289-296.
        Describes patterns of sleep apnea, insomnia, and hypersomnia in older adults. Reports that the incidence of life-threatening sleep apnea is twice as great in older adults who sleep less than four or more than ten hours per night. Discusses this phenomenon in terms of life expectancy.

PH5     Feinberg, I. (1974). Changes in sleep cycle patterns with age. Journal of Psychiatric Research, 10, 283-306.
        Describes the changes in sleep cycle patterns that change with age. In particular, amount and patterning of sleep in the older adult is related to the overall decrease in sleep-related EEG slow waves during stage IV sleep, decrease in the frequency, amplitude, and overall amount of alpha wave activity, and the poor formation, infrequency, and lower amplitude of sleep spindles.

PH6     Iragui, V. J., Kutas, M., Mitchener, M. R., & Hillyard, S. A. (1993). Effects of aging on event-related brain potentials and reaction times in an auditory oddball task. Psychophysiology, 30, 10-22.
        Examined the reaction times and latency, amplitude, and distributions of major auditory event-related potentials in 71 adults aged 18-82. Reaction time did not show significant slowing with age. Linear age-related decays in latency were found for endogenous event-related potential components that occur later in the standard sequence of event-related potentials.

PH7     Jarvik, L. F. (1988). Aging of the brain: How can we prevent it? The Gerontologist, 28, 739-747.
        Highlights normal vs. pathological aging related changes in intellect with a discussion of the genetic basis for dementia. Readable, but requires some background in behavioral genetics.

PH8     Jennings, J. R., Nabas, R., Brock, K. (1988). Memory retrieval in noise and psychophysiological response in the young and old. Psychophysiology, 25, 633-644.

Measured the cardiovascular responses of young (aged 18-24) and older (aged 61-78) adults during a memory retrieval task in which acoustic noise was presented. Cardiac and vascular responses were found to be related to performance. The authors also suggest that these responses were related to attention and rehearsal. Noise and age independently increased the number of associatively cued recall errors relative to orthographically cued recall errors. The authors conclude that task processing induced supportive physiological changes. These data are in contrast to the commonly held belief that the arousal decrement experienced by older adults constrains performance.

PH9     De Jong, H. L., Kok, A., & Van Rooy, J. C. (1988). Early and late selection in young and old adults: An event-related potential study. Psychophysiology, 25, 657-671.

Examined event-related potentials of young (aged 18-24) and older (aged 65-75) adults during a visual selection and memory search task. No differences in processing were found between groups, although older adults made significantly more errors relative to younger adults. The authors suggest that event-related potentials are sensitive to high memory load and that their morphology indicates that older adults processed the task more superficially. The authors discuss their findings in the context of both the task used and the N2 wave as an indicator of automatic mismatch detection.

PH10    Mancil, G. L. & Owsley, C. (1988). "Vision through my aging eyes": Revisited. Journal of the American Optometric Association, 59, 288-294.

Presents an overview of the psychophysiological, neuroanatomical, and physiological changes that occur in the aging eye. Reviews earlier research. Particular emphasis on reduced contrast sensitivity, difficulty seeing temporally modulated targets, deterioration of far periphery, and increase in intraocular light scatter.

PH11    Marsh, G. R. & Thompson, L. W. (1977). Psychophysiology of aging. In J. E. Birren & K. W. Schaie (Eds.), Handbook of the psychology of aging. New York: Van Nostrand Reinhold.

Classic chapter describes the development of the study of psychophysiology of aging, focusing primarily on the underarousal theory of aging, which was the predominant psychophysiological aging theory at the time. Reviews literature reporting studies on galvanic skin response, EEG, and heart rate reactivity in older adults.

PH12    Miles, L .E. & Dement, W. C. (1980). Sleep and aging. Sleep, 3,
        119-220.
            Describes the prominent features of aging as observed by EEG.
        States that the steady decrease in delta wave amplitude during slow
        wave sleep is the most conspicuous sign of the aged EEG. Also
        reports a linear increase in waking after sleep onset paralleled by an
        increase in the occurrence of brief arousal which are not perceived and
        may not cause actual wakefulness.

PH13    Miller, G. A., Bashore, T. R., Farwell, L. A., & Donchin, E. (1987).
        Research in geriatric psychophysiology. In K. W. Schaie (Ed.),
        Annual review of gerontology and geriatrics: V. 7 (pp. 1-28). New
        York: Springer.
            This chapter deals with the psychological implications of psycho-
        physiological changes with aging. The specific focus is on the
        cognitive manifestations of both normal and abnormal psychophysiolog-
        ical change.

PH14    Prinz, P. N. & Halter, J. B. (1981). Sleep disturbances in the aged:
        Some hormonal correlates and some newer therapeutic considerations.
        In C. Eisdorfer & E. Fann (Eds.), Psychopharmacology of aging.
        New York: S. P. Medical and Scientific Books.
            Describes significant correlations between plasma norepinephrine
        and sleep patterns in healthy males in their twenties and sixties. Older
        adults showed surges of norepinephrine in plasma following awakening
        by a loud tone, whereas younger subjects did not. The authors argue
        for development of a pharmacologic regimen to counteract sympathetic
        activity and improve sleep quality in aged adults.

PH15    Webb, W. B. & Dreblow, L. M. (1982). A modified method for
        scoring slow wave sleep of older subjects. Sleep, 5, 195-199.
            Reports that in addition to the decrease in amplitude of delta wave
        observed during slow wave sleep in elderly subjects, overall decreases
        in the absolute amount of delta wave activity is also observed.
        However, the authors point out that the significant age differences
        observed in this wave frequency are due to amplitude differences rather
        than in prevalence differences.

PH16    Welford, A. T. (1965). Performance, biological mechanisms, and
        age: A theoretical sketch. In A. T. Welford & J. E. Birren (Eds.),
        Behavior, aging and the nervous system. Springfield, IL: Charles C.
        Thomas.
            One of the first articulations of the overarousal theory of aging.
        Points to clinical and everyday observations that suggest that older

adults are hyperaroused, resulting in heightened activity, tension, and anxiety. Support for the theory is provided by studies of lipid mobilization, a measure of autonomic arousal, which is increased in older adults relative to younger adults during task performance.

PH17   Woodruff, D. S. (1985). Arousal, sleep, and aging. In J. E. Birren & K. W. Schaie (Eds.), Handbook of the psychology of aging (2nd ed.) (pp. 261-295). New York: Van Nostrand Reinhold.

Summarizes much of the literature on psychophysiological correlates of aging. Focuses on psychophysiological measures, such as electroencephalography and event-related potential measurement, as well as neurophysiological and neuroanatomic processes in aging. Discusses research in sleep and arousal using electrophysiological measures, and recommends areas for future research.

PH18   Woodruff-Pak, D. S. (1989). Longevity. In V. L. Bengston, K. W. Schaie (Eds.), The course of later life: Research and reflections (pp. 107-134). New York: Springer.

Examines classical conditioning as a model to study the aging organism. Places particular emphasis on the human and animal eyelid response as a paradigm for the investigation of the central nervous system and neural mechanisms of learning and memory. Discusses the relevance of the septohippocampal and cerebellar systems in learning and memory.

PH19   Woodruff-Pak, D. S. (1993). Neural plasticity as a substrate for cognitive adaptation in adulthood and aging. In J. Carella, J. M. Rybash, W. Hoyer, & M.L. Commons (Eds.), Adult information processing: Limits on loss (pp.13-35). San Diego: Academic Press.

Discusses the aging nervous system as a substrate for preserved or enhanced cognitive function in later life. Examines plasticity with regard to nervous system function in later life. Particularly emphasizes environmental enrichment and training and adaptation in neural/synaptic degeneration. Also examines the relatively recent development of pharmacologic cognitive-enhancers, such as nootropic compounds, cholinergic-enhancing agents, hormones, and neurotrophic drugs.

PH20   Woodruff-Pak, D. S., & Thompson, R. F. (1988). Cerebellar correlates of classical conditioning across the life span. In P. B. Baltes, D. L. Featherman & R. L. Lerner (Eds.), Life-span development and behavior: V. 9 (pp. 2-39). Hillsdale, NJ: Lawrence Erlbaum.

Explores comparative data on neurobiology and associative learning in light of a model of the classical conditioning of the eyelid response.

# 4

# *Sensation and Perception*

SP1    Barr, R., Giambra, L. (1990). Age-related decrement in selective
       auditory attention. Psychology and Aging, 5, 597-599.
       Even when minimizing the attentional demands of an auditory
       information processing task, age deficits in attention were obtained. As
       target uncertainty was ruled out, search deficits as a source of such
       performance are unlikely as an explanation.

SP2    Charness, N., & Bosman, E. A. (1990). Human factors and design for
       older adults. Handbook of the psychology of aging (pp. 446-464).
       New York: Academic Press.
       Examines person-environment relationships in later life, focusing on
       the older adult as a processor of information in the visual, auditory and
       spatial aspects of the environment.

SP3    Clark, J. E., Lanphear, A. K., & Riddick, C. C. (1987). The effects
       of video game playing on the response selection processing of elderly
       adults. Journal of Gerontology, 42, 82-85.
       Highlights the role of central processing deficits in reaction time,
       focusing on the initiation of a response in deciding to respond to a
       stimulus.

SP4    Czaja, S., & Glascock, A. (1994). Special Issue: Human factors and
       the aging driver. Experimental Aging Research, 20, 1-70.
       A comprehensive examination of those factors bearing on the driving
       performance of older adults. Topics include vehicular design, visual,
       perceptual, and psychomotor performance factors, and safety-mobility
       issues.

SP5     Digiovanna, A. G. (1994).  Human aging: Biological perspectives.
        New York: McGraw-Hill.
             Excellent overview of aging-related changes in a variety of body
        systems to include vision, audition, central nervous sytem, somesthesis,
        gustation and olfaction.  Well written and very readable.

SP6     Ferrini, A. F., & Ferrini, R. L. (1993).  Health in the later years.
        Dubuque, IA: William C. Brown.
             Broad-based text focusing on a variety of aspects of health-related
        issues as they relate to older adults.  Includes specific discussions of the
        aging of the nervous and sensory systems.

SP7     Fozard, J. L. (1990).  Vision and hearing in aging.  In J. E. Birren &
        K. W. Schaie (Eds.), Handbook of the psychology of aging (pp. 150-
        171).  New York: Academic Press.
             This chapter examines aging-related changes in the major sensory
        abilities, with implications for perceptual functioning.

SP8     Fozard, J. L., Vercruyssen, M., Reynolds, S. L., Hancock, P.A., &
        Quilter, R. E. (1994).  Age differences and changes in reaction time:
        The Baltimore longitudinal study of aging.  Journal of Gerontology:
        Psychological Sciences, 49, 179-189.
             Reports on cross-sectional and longitudinal analyses of simple and
        complex reaction time in persons aged 17-96.  Clear age and gender
        effects in performance were found, as well as increased variability of
        performance with age.

SP9     Howx, P. J., Jolles, J., & Vreeling, F. W. (1993).  Stroop interfer-
        ences:  Aging effects assessed with the Stroop Color-Word Test.
        Experimental Aging Research, 19, 209-224.
             In a cross sectional comparison of young and older adults, the ability
        to alter perceptual set was found to vary not only by age, but also by
        the extent to which persons had experienced biologically-relevant
        environmental events thought to impair brain functioning.  In addition,
        more highly educated persons performed more adequately.  Illustrative
        of the importance of the many factors bearing on perceptual function-
        ing, in addition to chronological age per se.

SP10    Kausler, D. F. (1991).  Sensory psychology and perception.  In D. E.
        Kausler (Ed.), Experimental psychology, cognition, and human aging
        (pp. 71-133).  New York:  Springer-Verlag.
             Well written, comprehensive overview of research on the sensory
        and perceptual aspects of psychological aging, from a psychophysical
        and signal detection perspective.  Includes discussions of the major

senses as well as a variety of perceptual processes, e.g., depth
perception, illusion magnitude, stimulus persistence, pattern recognition.

SP11    Kline, D. W., Kline, T., Fozard, J. L., Kocnik, W., Schieber, F., &
        Sekuler, R. (1992).  Vision, aging, and driving: The problems of older
        drivers. Journal of Gerontology: Psychological Sciences, 47, P27-P34.
            A nicely crafted article extending what we know about vision and
        aging to the driving environment of older adults.  Older persons
        reported a variety of visual difficulties in both everyday life and in
        driving. These factors may help to explain auto accidents among older
        drivers.

SP12    Kline, D. W., & Schieber, F. (1985).  Vision and aging.  In J. E.
        Birren & K. W. Schaie (Eds.), Handbook of the psychology of aging
        (pp. 296-331).  New York: Van Nostrand Reinhold.
            This review chapter discusses information processing in light of
        stimulus persistence, highlighting the distinction between age-related
        functioning in sustained vs. transient neural channels.

SP13    Kosnik, W., Winslow, L., Kline, D., Pensinki, K., & Sekular, R.
        (1988).  Visual changes in daily life throughout adulthood. Journal of
        Gerontology: Psychological Sciences, 43, 63-70.
            Excellent paper examining the self-reported visual difficulties of an
        everyday nature and their implications for functional ability in
        adulthood and later life.

SP14    Kozma, A., & Stones, M. J. (1990).  Decrements in habitual and
        maximal physical performance with age.  In K. W. Schaie (Ed.),
        Annual review of gerontology and geriatrics: V. 7 (pp. 1-24).  New
        York: Springer.
            Examines the literature on physical performance and aging drawing
        on studies of fitness, activity, reaction time, and record performance.

SP15    Long, G. M., & Crambert, R. F. (1990).  The nature and basis of age-
        related changes in dynamic visual activity. Psychology and Aging, 5,
        138-143.
            Examined young and old adults' ability to track moving targets,
        finding superior performance in the young.  These age effects are
        reduced by adjustments in ambient light levels.

SP16    Madden, D. J. (1990).  Adult age differences in the time course of
        visual attention. Journal of Gerontology: Psychological Sciences, 45,
        9-16.

This study found increased reaction time as a function of the distance of a target in a visual distance from a fixation point and of the presence of nontarget letters, suggesting a generalized slowing of visual processing and a deficit in learning to attend to visual targets in the presence of distractors.

SP17    Panek, P. E., Barrett, G. v., Sterns, H. L., & Alexander, R. A. (1977). A review of age changes in perceptual information processing ability with regard to driving. Experimental Aging Research, 3, 387-449.

Describes a model of information processing that while applied to older drivers, can be generalized to other real life situations.

SP18    Plude, D. J., Hoyer, W. J. (1986). Age and the selectivity of visual information processing. Psychology and Aging, 1, 4-10.

In responding to a visual display, nontarget stimuli executed a greater disruptive effect on performance in older adults, confirming that the magnitude of the divided attention deficit increases with age, whereas focused attention age deficits are minimal.

SP19    Ponds, R. W., Brouwer, W. H., & Van Wolffelaar, P. C. (1988). Adult age differences in divided attention in a simulated driving task. Journal of Gerontology: Psychological Sciences, 43, 151-156.

In a simulated driving task, even when adjusting for simple task performance, older persons showed impaired ability to divide attention in a task design to mimic everyday driving.

SP20    Slawinski, E. B., Hartel, D. M., & Kline, D. W. (1993). Self-reported hearing problems in daily life throughout adulthood. Psychology and Aging, 8, 552-561.

Interesting study dealing with self-reported hearing difficulties by adults aged 20-94. It suggested that a variety of problems related to speech perception were most common with increased age, especially for those who rated their hearing as poor in quality.

SP21    Spirduso, W. W., & McRae, P. G. (1990). Motor performance and aging. Handbook of the psychology of aging (pp. 184-220). New York: Academic Press.

Intrinsic factors of motor performance such as work capacity, muscular strength and psychomotor speed as they relate to older persons performance is discussed, as are interventions to enhance such performance.

SP22    Whitbourne, S. K. (1985). The aging body: Physiological changes and psychological consequences. New York: Springer-Verlag.

Excellent, though somewhat dated detailing of sensory system changes with age and the psychological implications. The aging of major sensory systems is discussed in detail. Well referenced.

SP23    Wilkinson, R. T., & Allison, S. (1989). Age and simple reaction time: Decade differences for 5,325 subjects. Journal of Gerontology: Psychological Sciences, 44, 29-36.

This extensive study reports mean age differences and age effects in the variability of simple reaction time.

# 5

# *Learning and Memory*

L1    Allen, P. A., & Coyne, A. C. (1988). Age differences in primary organization or processing variability? Part I: an examination of age and primary organization. Experimental Aging Research, 14, 143-149.

    Argues for the existence of a lower level of subjective memory organization called primary organization. Presumably, primary organization occurs automatically and unconsciously and is based on item order.

L2    Basden, B. H., Basden, D. R., & Bartlett, K. (1993). Memory organization in elderly subjects. Experimental Aging Research, 19, 29-38.

    This study investigated the influence of the accessibility of retrieval cues on younger and older adults' memory for unrelated words, finding little facilitative effect on age-related performance differences. The authors highlight the roles of item-specific vs. relational processing in discussing their findings.

L3    Cavanaugh, J. C., Grady, J. G., & Perlmutter, M. (1983). Forgetting and use of memory aids in 20 to 70 year olds everyday life. International Journal of Aging and Human Development, 17, 113-122.

    Subjects kept a daily record of their failures to remember things such as an item they had intended to purchase at the supermarket. Older subjects were much more concerned about memory failures, though the actual number of memory failures was only moderately greater than the number of memory failures reported by younger subjects.

L4        Cerella, J. (1990). Aging and information-processing rate. Handbook of the psychology of aging (pp. 201-221). New York: Academic Press.
          Recent theory and data dealing with information processing rate and aging from a neural network perspective, emphasizing breakdown among interconnections with aging leading to greater response latency.

L5        Cerella, J., Rybash, J., Hoyer, W. L., & Commons, M. L. (1993). Adult information processing: Limits on loss. New York: Academic Press.
          This volume contains chapters by leading researchers in cognitive aging, emphasizing a theme of perserved functioning. Different sections focus on diverse aspects of information processing such as its neurological basis, rates of processing, attention object and word perception, language comprehension and learning, memory and problem solving.

L6        Cockburn, B., & Smith, J. (1991). The relative influence of intelligence and age on everyday memory. Journal of Gerontology: Psychological Sciences, 46, 31-36.
          This study found that fluid ability predicted performance on most memory tasks, and that age predicted both prospective and verbal memory performance independent of intelligence. Levels of activity, but not crystallized skill also predicted performance.

L7        Cohen, G. (1989). Memory in the real world. Hove and London: Lawrence Erlbaum Associates.
          Provides a comprehensive review of studies investigating different forms of rehearsal-independent memory, such as memory for activities, actions, and content of conversational context.

L8        Cohen, G., & Faulkner, D. (1989). Age differences in source forgetting: Effects on reality monitoring and on eyewitness testimony. Psychology and Aging, 4, 10-17.
          In another investigation of performed versus imagined actions, these researchers found a much larger effect of accurate judgment for younger subjects relative to older subjects.

L9        Cornelius, S. W. & Caspi, A. (1987). Everyday problem solving in adulthood and old age. Psychology and Aging, 2, 144-153.
          Adults aged 20 to 70 years were compared on everyday problem solving tasks and a reasoning task. A positive linear relationship was found for age and everyday problem solving scores. A statistically significant correlation between the two task types was also reported.

L10    Craik, F.I.M., & Salthouse, T. A. (1992). <u>Handbook of aging and cognition</u>. Hillsdale, NJ: Lawrence Erlbaum.
       Examination of distinct aspects of cognitive aging by various authors, to include chapters on neuropsychology and memory, physiology and cognition, dementia as well as a section on applied cognitive aging. Excellent scientific reference.

L11    Czaja, S., & Glascock, A. (1994). Special issue: Technology and environmental issues for the elderly. <u>Experimental Aging Research</u>, <u>20</u>, 173-244.
       This volume addresses older persons' needs for safety, rehabilitation, supportive environmental designs and technology that will enhance everyday functional skills.

L12    Denny, N. W. (1979). Problem solving in later adulthood: Intervention research. In P. B. Baltes, D. L. Featherman & R. L. Lerner (Eds.), <u>Life-span development and behavior: V 2</u> (pp. 38-67). New York: Academic Press.
       Discusses early cognitive intervention research in light of the manipulation of capacity vs. strategy variables as a means of improving performance.

L13    Denney, N. W. (1989). Everyday problem solving: Methodological issues, research, and a model. In L. W. Poon, D. C. Rubin, & B. A. Wilson (Eds.), <u>Everyday cognition in adulthood and late life</u>. New York: Cambridge University Press.
       This prolific researcher in the area of everyday cognition reviews her own findings as well as others', based on the premise that research with appropiate and relavant tools is more informative than standard laboratory tasks. Also argues that performance deficits seen in the laboratory might be task- rather than age-related.

L14    Denney, N. W. & Palmer, M. (1981). Adult age differences on traditional and practical problem-solving measures. <u>Journal of Gerontology</u>, <u>36</u>, 323-328.
       One of the first systematic examinations of everyday problem-solving. Subjects ranging from their 20s to 70s responded to practical situational questions. Scores tended to peak for subjects in ther 40s and 50s, with the older subjects scoring as well as subjects in their 20s. Results are discussed in terms of the difference in the exercise of these skills needed to maintain them.

L15    Dobbs, A. R., & Rule, B. G. (1989). Adult age differences in working memory. <u>Psychology and Aging</u>, <u>4</u>, 500-503.

Examined performance on active and passive memory tasks in adults ranging in age from 30 to 99 years. Age differences were not pronounced for the passive memory task. Declines were found, however, for the working memory task for adults over the age of 60 years. The authors attribute the observed differences to a decrease in processing flexibility with age.

L16    Dror, I. E., & Kosslyn, S. M. (1994). Mental imagery and aging. Psychology and Aging, 9, 90-102.
       Young and old adults performed several mental imagery tasks. While there was some decline with age in the ability to maintain images, elderly persons were able to compose and scan visual mental images as well as young adults.

L17    Duchek, J. M (1984). Encoding and retrieval differences between the young and old: The impact of attentional capacity usage. Developmental Psychology, 20, 1173-1180.
       Found that older adults reponded better to semantically related cue that to semantically unrelated cues on a category retrieval task, in support of the encoding specificity principle. Younger subjects performed substantially better than older subjects, however.

L18    Durkin, M., Prescott, L., Furchgott, E., Cantor, J., & Powell, D. A. (1993). Concommitant eyeblink and heart rate classical conditioning in young, middle aged, and elderly human subjects. Psychology and Aging, 8, 571-581.
       Compared adults of varying ages in terms of their likelihood of acquiring classically conditioned eyeblink and heart rate responses. While those exposed to Pavlovian procedures were more likely than controls to acquire the CR, there was a clear age-related impairment in general associative ability.

L19    Elias, P. K., Elias, M. F., Robbins, M. A., & Gage, P. (1987). Acquisition of word processing skills by younger, middle aged and older adults. Psychology and Aging, 2, 340-348.
       Adults of varying ages were trained to word process. While all persons acquired such skills, older adults took longer to complete training and evaluation and performed more poorly on a skills review exam.

L20    Erber, J. T., Szuchman, L. T., & Rothberg, S. T. (1990). Everyday memory failure: Age differences in appraisal and attribution. Psychology and Aging, 5, 236-241.

Data from young and older adults confirmed a double standard used to explain memory failure in the young and old. Both target age and perceived age were important to explaining such failures to the detriment of older age targets.

L21   Flynn, T. M., & Storandt, M. (1990). Supplemental group discussions in memory training for older adults. Psychology and Aging, 5, 178-181.

   The authors discuss the limits of self-taught mnemonics in improving learning efficiency. They report that self-instruction is only effective when it is supplemented by periodic group discussions about the mnemonic strategies.

L22   Guttentag, R. E., & Hunt, R. R.. (1988). Adult age differences in memory for imagined and performed actions. Journal of Gerontology, 43, 107-108.

   Found that younger subjects recall significantly more of both performed and imagined actions than elderly subjects. Younger subjects were also significantly more accurate in judging whether each action had been performed or imagined, although this effect was slight.

L23   Hertzog, C., Dixon, r. A., & Hultsch, D. F. (1990). Relationships between metamemory, memory predictions and memory task performance. Psychology and Aging, 5, 215-227.

   In highlighting the importance of metamemorial skills in late life, these researchers found older persons had poorer memory and that memory self efficacy predicted poorer memory performances.

L24   Hess, T. (1990). Aging and cognition: Knowledge, organization and utilization. Amsterdam: North-Holland

   This edited volume approaches cognition from a context-specific perspective emphasizing the acquired expertise many older persons possess. Chapters deal with topics ranging from metamemory, expertise, visual information processing, everyday intelligence, and real world problem solving.

L25   Hasher, L., & Zacks, R. T. (1988). Working memory, comprehension, and aging: A review and a new view. In G. Bower (Ed.), The psychology of learning and motivation (pp. 192-225). San Diego, CA: Academic Press.

   Classic paper discussing the hypothesis that it is the impairment of the ability to suppress irrelevant information that accounts for information processing, memory, and language comprehension deficits in aged persons.

L26    Hayslip, B., Kennelly, K., & Maloy, R. (1990). Fatigue, depression,
       and cognitive performance among aged persons. <u>Experimental Aging
       Reseasrch</u>, <u>16</u>, 111-115.
             Found that those elders who were more depressed were more
       susceptible to fatigue which in turn was associated with poorer short
       term memory performance.

L27    Hultsch, D. F., & Dixon, R. A. (1984). Memory for text materials in
       adulthood. In P. B. Baltes & O. G. Brim, Jr. (Eds.), <u>Life-span
       development and behavior V. 6</u> (pp. 78-110). New York: Academic
       Press.
             Describes the authors' program of research investigating memory for
       text materials in light of the shortcomings that they identify in such
       work to date.

L28    Hultsch, D. F., & Dixon, R. A. (1990). Learning and memory in
       aging. <u>Handbook of the psychology of aging</u> (pp. 259-274). New
       York: Academic Press.
             Reviews evidence for aging-related declines in diverse memory
       systems and memory processes, as well as exploring questions of the
       impact of experience and interventions on memory function.

L29    Jackson, J. D., & Kemper, S. (1993). Age differences in summarizing
       descriptive and procedural texts. <u>Experimental Aging Research</u>, <u>19</u>,
       39-51.
             In a study of text processing, these authors found that when
       presented with two different types of expository texts to read and
       summarize, older adults produced more total and central ideas than
       young adults, despite reading more slowly.

L30    Kausler, D. F. (1991). Attention. In D. F. Kausler (Ed.), <u>Experimen-
       tal psychology, cognition, and human aging</u> (pp. 134-188). New York:
       Springer-Verlag.
             Comprehensively reviews the aging literature in vigilance, selective
       attention and divided attention. Excellent resource.

L31    Kausler, D. F. (1991). Episodic memory: Effortful phenomena. In D.
       F. Kausler (Ed.), <u>Experimental psychology, cognition, and human
       aging</u> (pp. 365-430)). New York: Springer-Verlag.
             This chapter focuses on organizational processes, encoding,
       retrieval, prospective memory, and memory for discourse, all of which
       require effortful rehearsal.

L32     Kausler, D. F. (1991). Generic memory: Internal lexicon, implicit memory, metamemory. In D. F. Kausler (Ed.), Experimental psychology, cognition, and human aging (pp. 490-551). New York: Springer-Verlag.
        Discusses acquired knowledge systems as well as knowledge about one's memory as a function of age.

L33     Kausler, D. F. (1991). Learning: Conditioning, instrumental, motor skill, procedural. In D. F. Kausler (Ed.), Experimental psychology, cognition, and human aging (pp. 189-238). New York: Springer-Verlag.
        Excellent overview of age differences in the more elemental aspects of learning processes. Includes a discussion of abnormal aging.

L34     Kausler, D. F. (1991). Learning: Verbal learning, mnemonics, transfer. In D. F. Kausler (Ed.), Experimental psychology, cognition, and human aging (pp. 239-291). New York: Springer-Verlag.
        Well-done discussion of classical verbal learning aging research to include paired associate and serial learning, the use of mnemonic aids, transfer, and both normal and abnormal aging.

L35     Kausler, D. F. (1991). Memory: Models of episodic memory and related research issues. In D. F. Kausler (Ed.), Experimental psychology, cognition, and human aging (pp. 292-364). New York: Springer-Verlag.
        Discusses memory systems and several approaches to conceptualizing episodic memory.

L36     Kausler, D. F. (1991). Rehearsal-independent episodic memory: Long-term forgetting. In D. F. Kausler (Ed.), Experimental psychology, cognition, and human aging (pp. 431-489). New York: Springer-Verlag.
        Discusses the many dimensions of episodic memory that are automatic in nature such as the encoding of the frequency of events or temporal memory for events.

L37     Kausler, D. F. (1991). Thinking: Concept formation and identification. In D. F. Kausler (Ed.), Experimental psychology, cognition, and human aging (pp. 552-595). New York: Springer-Verlag.
        Discusses classical literature as well as newer research in concept formation and acquisition.

L38     Kausler, D. F. (1991). Thinking: Problem solving and reasoning. In
        D. F. Kausler (Ed.), <u>Experimental psychology, cognition, and human
        aging</u> (pp. 596-656.). New York: Springer-Verlag.
                Well done treatment of an understudied aspect of cognitive aging.
        Includes diverse types of reasoning tasks and recent problem solving
        research.

L39     Kausler, D. H. (1994). <u>Learning and memory in normal aging</u>. San
        Diego, CA: Academic Press.
                Extremely well-done and up-to-date presentation of the scientific
        literature on aging, learning, and memory. While very technical in
        nature, findings are clearly explained and research well integrated.
        Excellent resource.

L40     Lachman, M., Weaver, S., Bandura, M., Elliot, E., & Lewkowicz, C.
        J. (1992). Improving memory and control beliefs through cognitive
        restructuring and self-generated strategies. <u>Journal of Gerontology:
        Psychological Sciences</u>, <u>47</u>, P293-P299.
                Using a combination of cognitive restructuring and memory skills
        training, older persons' perceptions of their control over memory and
        their ability to improve their memory. Suggests that skill availability
        and expectations about memory loss and aging are critical aspects of
        older persons' perceptions of their memory skills.

L41     Lichty, W., Kausler, D. H., & Martinez, D. R. (1986). Adult age
        differences in memory for motor versus cognitive activities. <u>Experi-
        mental Aging Research</u>, <u>12</u>, 227-230.
                Found that older adults recalled significantly more about the motor
        tasks than the cognitive tasks they had engaged in, although there was
        a significant age-related memory deficit for both types of tasks.
        Possible mechanisms for the disparity are discussed.

L42     Light, L. (1990). Interactions between memory and language in old
        age. <u>Handbook of the psychology of aging</u> (pp. 275-290). New York:
        Academic Press.
                Explores the basis for declines in memory with age based on deficits
        in language comprehension, emphasizing the mutual relationship among
        the two.

L43     Light, L. L. , & Burke, D. M. (Eds). (1989). <u>Language, memory,
        and aging</u>. New York: Cambridge University Press.
                This is a detailed, technical account of interactions between language
        function and memory with aging. Individual chapters are brief but

comprehensive. Recommended only for those with some background in cognition.

L44    Lorsbach, T. C., & Simpson, G. B. (1988). Dual-task performance as a function of adult age and task complexity. Psychology and Aging, 3, 210-212.
       Utilizing a dual task paradigm, it was found that older persons' performance was slower in tasks varying in complexity requiring letter matching, especially for the retrieval and comparison of letters. Results suggest an impairment of such skills with age where divided attention allocation is required.

L45    Luszez, M. A., Roberts, T. H., & Mattiske, J. K. (1990). Use of relational and item-specific information in remembering by younger and older adults. Psychology and Aging, 5, 242-249.
       Found that elderly subjects benefit from engaging in deep processing of individual words and thinking about inter-word relationships in terms of episodic memory function.

L46    McDowd, J. M., & Birren, J. E. (1990). Aging and attentional processes. Handbook of the psychology of aging (pp. 222-233). New York: Academic Press.
       This chapter focuses on the impact of aging on attentional processes such as divided attention, selective attention and sustained attention.

L47    O'Hara, M. W., Hinnicks, J. V., Kohout, F. J., Wallace, R. B., & Lemke, J. H. (1986). Memory complaint and memory performance in depressed elderly. Psychology and Aging, 1, 208-214.
       Reinforces empirically the clinical observation that depressed elderly complain more often about memory loss, relative to actual memory losses, whose magnitude is slight in such persons.

L48    Parkinson, S. R., Lindholm, J. M., & Inman, V. W. (1982). An analysis of age differences in immediate recall. Journal of Gerontology, 37, 425-431.
       Measured the extent of recency effect in free recall protocols using a number of procedures. The authors report an age-related loss in the magnitude of the recency effect by as much as 20%, relative to young adults.

L49    Patton, G. W. R., & Meit, M. (1993). Effect of aging on prospective and incidental memory. Experimental Aging Research, 19, 165-176.
       This series of three studies explored age differences in prospective and incidental memory performance, subject to the availability of

external memory aids. Not only were external aids more effective to older persons' prospective performance, but their greater motivation to complete the task was important as well. Young adults demonstrated superior incidental memory.

L50    Perlmutter, M. (1986). A life span view of memory. In P. B. Baltes, D. L. Featherman & R. L. Lerner (Eds.), Life-span development and behavior: V 7 (pp. 272-313). Hillsdale, NJ: Lawrence Erlbaum.
       This chapter reviews available research on memory systems and memory processes from a life span perspective, emphasizing distinct types of change in components of memory and their adaptive value.

L51    Poon, L. W. (Ed.). (1986). Handbook for clinical memory assess-ment of older adults. Washington DC: American Psychological Association.
       This edited volume attempts to integrate clinical problems of memory research with rigorous experimental approaches in aging and memory research. Includes explication of many different instruments for assessing memory performance, and makes a particular contribution in discussing differences between dementia and depression in older adults.

L52    Poon, L. W., Rubin, D. C., & Wilson, B. A. (1989). Everyday cognition in adulthood in late life. Cambridge: Cambridge University Press.
       This edited volume brings together research on applied cognition in adulthood. Includes chapters on theory and lab vs. real world research, text processing, speech comprehension, spatial memory and comprehen-sion, metamemory, as well as an extensive section on intervention.

L53    Puckett, J. M., & Sockburger, D. W. (1988). Absence of age-related proneness to short-term retroactive interference in the absence of rehearsal. Psychology and Aging, 3, 324-347.
       Examined short-term forgetting for older versus younger adults. Identified subjects who surrepititiously engaged in rehearsal of to-be-remembered words while engaging in a distractor task. For young and older subjects identified as non-rehearsers, no difference in rate of forgetting was observed.

L54    Puglisi, J. T., Park, D. C., Smith, A. D., & Dudley, W. N. (1988). Age differences in encoding specificity. Journal of Gerontology: Psychological Sciences, 43, 145-150.
       Tested the encoding specificity principle by pairing weakly associated words with target words on a study trial and then either

reinstated them as retrieval cues or replaced them with strongly associated words on a cued-recall test trial. Results failed to support the differential operation of encoding specificity.

L55 Rabinowitz, J. C. (1984). Aging and recognition failure. Journal of Gerontology, 41, 368-375.

Replicated Tulving and Thompson's (1973) study, using older and younger adults. Results only partially supported the theory that retrieval deficits in aging are influenced by contextual encoding ability.

L56 Rabinowitz, J. C., & Craik, F. I. M. (1986). Prior retrieval effects in young and old adults. Journal of Gerontology, 41, 368-375.

Reports that memory for items to be retrieved is better if those items have been previously retrieved. Young adults outperformed older adults; however, the pattern of results was the same for both groups. The authors suggest that retrieval practice may be an effective mnemonic technique that can be easily taught to older adults.

L57 Randt, C. T., Brown, E. R., & Osborne, D. P. (1980). A memory test for longitudinal measurement of mild to moderate deficits. Clinical Neuropsychology, 2, 184-194.

Recall of short stories were tested immediately and 24 hours after presentation. Recall for activites performed while participating in the study was also measured. Results suggest that the ability to recall meaningful information decreases with age in a linear manner.

L58 Rose, T. L., & Yesavage, J. A. (1983). Differential effects of a list-learning mnemonic in three groups. Gerontology, 29, 293-298.

Examined the effectiveness of the method of loci mnemonic on recall of items. Older adults receiving training performed better than controls but worse than similarly trained young-adult subjects.

L59 Rybash, J. M., Hoyer, W. J., & Roodin, P. A. (1986) Adult cognition and aging: Processing, thinking, and knowing. New York: Pergamon Press.

This is a thoughtful lifespan developmental approach to understanding changes in cognition in late adulthood. It is a relatively brief volume, and emphasizes complex cognitive processes utilizing both Piagetian and cognitive science approaches.

L60 Salthouse, T. A. (1989). Age-related changes in basic cognitive processes. In M. Storandt & G. R. VandenBos (Eds), The adult years: Continuity and change. Washington DC: American Psychological Association.

Describes the major issues involved in the topic of cognitive change with age, and summarizes relevant research in the area in an historical context. Discusses aspects of cognition that have reliably been found to change with age as well as those which have not. Critically examines results from various studies of aging and cognition.

L61     Salthouse, T. A. (1991). Theoretical perspectives on cognitive aging. Hillsdale, NJ: Lawrence Erlbaum.

Critical discussion of adult cognition from the author's own theoretical perspective examining the relative merits of various explanations for aging-related shifts in cognitive performance.

L62     Salthouse, T. A. (1992). Why do adult age differences increase with task complexity? Developmental Psychology, 28, 905-918.

This study highlights the role that task complexity, as a reflection of working memory resources, plays in contributing to age differences in cognition.

L63     Salthouse, T. A. (1994). The nature of the influence of speed on adult age differences in cognition. Developmental Psychology, 30, 240-259.

This study explores the role of speed of processing in accounting for age effects in tasks assessing memory, reasoning, and spatial ability of both a speeded and an unspeeded nature.

L64     Salthouse, T. A., & Babcock, R. L. (1991). Decomposing adult age differences in working memory. Developmental Psychology, 27, 763-776.

These authors found that age differences in working memory were attenuated when controlled for the effects of storage capacity, efficiency of processing, coordination effectiveness and speed of comparison. Suggests aging is associated with a slowing of basic information processing ability.

L65     Salthouse, T. A., Kausler, D. H., & Saults, J. S. (1988). Investigation of student status, background variables, and the feasability of standard tasks in cognitive aging research. Psychology and Aging, 3, 29-37.

In a study of 233 adults who attempted to solve a variety of intellectual, memory, and learning tasks, it was found that college students are suspect as an age control group. Older adults performed as expected on the bases of expected age trends except for speeded performance.

L66     Sanders, R. E., Wise, J. L., Liddle, C. L., & Murphy, M. D. (1990). Adult age comparisons in the processing of event frequency information. Psychology and Aging, 5, 172-177.
        Proposes a nonoptimal model for frequency memory, in which encoding of frequency information requires minimal effort and little memory capacity to occur and produce memory scores better than chance performance. Also reports slightly better scores for older subjects relative to younger subjects.

L67     Scogin, F., & Bienias, J. L. (1988). A three-year follow-up of older adult participants in a memory skills training program. Psychology and Aging, 3, 334-337.
        This unique study investigates the long-term efficacy of memory skills traiing in terms of both memory performance and memory complaints.

L68     Squire, L. R. (1989). On the course of forgetting in very long-term memory. Journal of Experimental Psychology: Learning, Memory, and Cognition, 15, 241-245.
        Examined long-term retention for names of television shows that were aired for only one year. Reports about 20% forgetting for the first six years, with relatively little further forgetting for the next ten years, although the author reports a gradual linear decline in retention.

L69     Stigodotter-Nealy, A., & Bachman, L. (1993). Long-term maintenance of gains from memory training in older adults: Two 3 1/2 year follow-up studies. Journal of Gerontology: Psychological Sciences, 48, P233-P237.
        In a rare long term evaluation of a memory training program, maintenance of gains in performance obtained at a 6-month follow-up were obtained at a 3 1/2 year follow-up. Specific instruction in encoding seemed to be most positive, as are findings where the relationship between training and criterion tasks was the strongest.

L70     Storandt, M., Botwinick, J., & Danziger, W. L. (1986). Longitudinal changes: Patients with mild SDAT and matched healthy controls. In L. W. Poon (Ed.), Clinical memory assesment of older adults. Washington DC: American Psychological Association.
        Describes changes that occur in disease versus healthy aging. Studies are discussed in which the performance of Alzheimer's patients and healthy age-matched controls are compared for speed of responding, paired associate learning, and intelligence testing. Particularly emphasizes the marked deficits that occur over a short period of time in diseased patients.

L71     Treat, N. J., Poon, L. W., & Fozard, J. L. (1981). Age, imagery, and practice in paired-associate learning. Experimental Aging Research, 7, 337-342.

Report that nonspecific transfer occurred regardless of age, when six paired-associate lists were practiced to errorless criterion over three sessions, two weeks apart. Although more mean trials were required for older subjects relative to younger subjects at all three sessions, similar transfer occurred for both groups.

L72     Tulving, E. (1968). Theoretical issues in free recall. In T. R. Dixon & D. L. Horton (Eds.), Verbal behavior and general behavior theory. Englewood Cliffs, NJ: Prentice-Hall.

This classic work describes issues related to free recall, including a two-stage process explanation of retrieval of organized memory traces. Also discusses clustering, memory search, and levels of memory organization.

L73     Tulving, E. & Thomson, D. M. (1973). Encoding specificity and retrieval processes in episodic memory. Psychological Review, 80, 352-373.

Describes the encoding specificity principle of memory, which states that memory is best when the context or information available at encoding is also available at retrieval.

L74     Verhaeghen, P., Marcoen, A., & Goossens, L. (1992). Improving memory performance in the aged through mnemonic training: A meta-analytic study. Psychology and Aging, 7, 242-251.

Examines the effectiveness of mnemonics training, finding that efficacy related to age, length of training sessions, when persons were pretrained and to the specific nature of the training provided.

L75     Verhaeghen, P., Marcoen, A., & Goossens, L. (1993). Facts and fiction about memory aging: A quantitative integration of research findings. Journal of Gerontology: Psychological Sciences, 48, P151-P171.

In a meta-analysis of over 120 research studies, the authors concluded that age differences are quite large, favoring young adults in some aspects of memory (e.g., encoding), but not others (e.g., extracting main ideas, association strtategies). While reviewing material is more helpful for older adults, those with less education tend to score more poorly.

L76    West, R. L., Crook, T. H., & Barron, K. L. (1992). Everyday
       memory performance across the life span: Effects of age and noncog-
       nitive individual differences. Psychology and Aging, 7, 72-82.
           In over 2000 adults aged 18-90, age was found to best predict
       everyday memory performance. However, for some aspects of
       memory, vocabulary level and gender are also important predictors.

L77    West, R. L., & Sinnott, J. D. (1992). Everyday memory and aging:
       Current research and methodology. New York: Springer-Verlag.
           This edited volume contains chapters on a variety of methodological
       approaches to everyday memory and cognition, semantic memory,
       speech processing, intervention as well as theory-application relation-
       ships.

L78    Yesavage, J. A., & Rose, T. L. (1984). Semantic elaboration and the
       method of loci: A new trip for older learners. Experimental Aging
       Research, 10, 155-159.
           Described the results of a recall performance task following training
       of the method of loci mnemonic versus the method of loci in combina-
       tion with judgement ratings of the stimuli. Subjects who received the
       combination training performed better than subjects receiving method
       of loci training only. The positive effects of this type of training were
       observed following a dely, as well. The authors suggest that the
       judgment rating forced elaboration processes to occur, which enhanced
       memorial performance.

L79    Yesavage, J. A., & Rose, T. L. (1984). The effects of a face-name
       mnemonic in young, middle-aged, and elderly adults. Experimental
       Aging Research, 10, 55-57.
           Twelve face-name pairs were presented to young, middle-aged, and
       older subjects for study. A pretest consisted of presentation of the face
       list, where the subject was required to generate the name that had been
       paired with the face. Training consisted of experimenter-provided
       keyword to link the face with its corresponding name. A second face
       list was presented at posttest. Training was followed by a substantial
       increase in proportion of names recalled for all three age groups.
       However, an age-related decline in performance was noted for both
       pre- and posttest.

L80    Zelinski, E., Gilewski, M. J., & Schaie, K. W. (1993). Individual
       differences in cross-sectional and 3-year longitudinal memory perfor-
       mance. Psychology and Aging, 8, 176-186.
           These authors found that being retested, having higher intelligence,
       and being female predicted better prose recall and recognition

performance.  This argues for the importance of individual differences
in memory performance in later life.

L81      Zivian, M. T., & Darjes, R. W.  (1983).  Free recall by in-school and
         out-of-school adults:  Performance and memory.  Developmental
         Psychology, 19, 513-520.
             Report significantly more items recalled for younger adults
         compared to older adults in a non-cued category recall task.  Suggests
         that the encoding of specific instances is impaired with age, while the
         encoding of higher-order information may be age insensitive.

# 6

# *Intelligence*

I1    Anstey, K., Stankov, L., & Lord, S. (1993). Primary aging, secondary aging, and intelligence. Psychology and Aging, 8, 562-570.
      These authors found that innate maturation/sensorimotor variables and education, but not health, predicted age deficits in fluid ability. Both primary and secondary aging are therefore important in accounting for intellectual change.

I2    Baltes, P. B., Dittmann-Kohli, F., & Dixon, R. A. (1984). New perspectives on the development of intelligence in adulthood: Toward a dual-process conception and a model of selective optimization with compensation. In P. B. Baltes & O. G. Brim Jr. (Eds.), Life-span development and behavior: V. 6 (pp. 34-77). New York: Academic Press.
      Sets forth the senior author's ideas about the pragmatics vs. the mechanics of intelligence as well as the roles each play in helping persons adjust to the aging process.

I3    Baltes, P. B., Dittmann-Kohli, F., & Dliegl, R. (1986). Reserve capacity of the elderly in age-sensitive tests of fluid intelligence: Replication and extension. Psychology and Aging, 1, 172-177.
      This seminal training study supports the contention that training facilitates performance on fluid ability measures as reflections of the untapped reserve intellectual capacity of older adults.

I4    Berg, C. A. (1992). Perspectives for viewing intellectual development throughout the life course. In R. J. Sternberg & C. Berg (Eds.), Intellectual development (pp. 1-15).

Excellent presentation of very diverse theoretical perspectives on intelligence in adulthood and old age.

I5    Berg, C. A., Sternberg, R. J. (1992). Adults'conceptions of intelligence across the adult life span. Psychology and Aging, 7, 221-231.
      Views about intelligence help to determine future performance. Among adults, such views were characterized by the ability to deal with novelty, everyday competence, and verbal competence. Each was viewed as differentially important to persons of different ages by persons who varied in age. Amenability to change and multidimensionality also characterized such views.

I6    Berry, J. M. (1989). Cognitive efficacy: A life span developmental perspective. Developmental Psychology, 25, 683-735.
      This series of articles reports on various aspects of cognitive (memory, intellectual) self efficacy in adults. Excellent group of studies that includes both theory and research.

I7    Blackburn, J. A., & Papalia, D. E. (1992). The study of adult cognition from a Piagetian perspective. In R. J. Sternberg & C. Berg (Eds.), Intellectual development (pp. 141-160).
      Excellent review of Piagetian intelligence research in adulthood focusing on concrete and formal operations as well as extensions of such research into later life.

I8    Cornelius, S., & Caspi, A. (1987). Everyday problem solving in adulthood and old age. Psychology and Aging, 2, 144-153.
      Reports on the construction of a test of everyday problem solving, consisting of sex distinct content domains. Such scores were positively related to age, but independent of level of education.

I9    Denny, N. (1982). Aging and cognitive changes. In B. Wolman (Ed.), Handbook of developmental psychology (pp. 807-827). Englewood Cliffs, NJ: Prentice Hall.
      Differentiates exercised intellectual skills from optimally exercised ones, with differential change between the two being the greatest in late adulthood.

I10   Hayslip, B. (1989). Alternative mechanisms for improvements in fluid ability performance among aged persons. Psychology and Aging, 4, 122-124.
      Based on the author's contention that performance anxiety may negatively affect older adults' performance on measures of fluid ability, subjects were trained in stress inoculation following pretesting. The

investigator found that while stress inoculation training did not
significantly reduce scores in subjective measures of anxiety, posttest
performance on induction tasks was improved relative to controls.

I11    Hayslip, B. & Maloy, R. (1991). The interface between psychometric
       abilities and everyday intelligence. In R. West & J. Sinnott (Eds.),
       Everyday memory and aging. New York: Springer.
          Examined the effects of heuristics training on fluid ability and
       everyday tasks. Despite the correlation between these two types of
       tasks, the authors found no generalization of training to the everyday
       tasks. Training-specific fluid abilities were significantly improved
       following training, however.

I12    Hayslip, B., & Sterns, H. L. (1979). Age differences in relationships
       between crystallized and fluid intelligences and problem solving.
       Journal of Gerontology, 34, 404-414.
          Evaluated whether abstract or concrete information influenced
       performance on a concept identification task. While older adults
       performed more poorly than younger adults, the valence of the task was
       not found to impact performance significantly. Differential relation-
       ships between intelligence and problem solving were found across age
       groups.

I13    Hertzog, C. (1989). Influences of cognitive slowing on aging
       differences in intelligence. Developmental Psychology, 25, 636-651.
          This extensive cross-sectional study found that age differences in
       many types of cognitive abilities were attenuated when speed of
       performance was taken into account. These findings highlight the role
       of information-processing speed in intelligence across adulthood.

I14    Hertzog, C., & Schaie, K. W. (1986). Stability and change in adult
       intelligence: Analysis of longitudinal covariance structures. Psycholo-
       gy and Aging, 1, 159-171.
          A series of longitudinal factor analyses found complete invariance
       of PMA factor loadings on general ability. Individual differences in
       rank order of general ability were also stable over time.

I15    Horn, J. L. (1978). Human ability systems. In P. B. Baltes (Ed.),
       Life-span development and behavior: V. 1 (pp. 212-257). New York:
       Academic Press.
          Classic though dated chapter on the author's work reflecting the
       development of crystallized and fluid intelligences.

I16     Horn, J. L., & Hofer, S. M. (1992). Major abilities and development
        in the adult period. In R. J. Sternberg & C. Berg (Eds.), Intellectual
        development (pp. 44-99).
                Latest discussion regarding the senior author's research in crystal-
        lized and fluid intelligences as well as a more general treatment of
        other perspectives on intelligence in adulthood.

I17     Hultsch, D. F., Hammer, M., & Small, B. J. (1993). Age differences
        in cognitive performance in later life: Relationships to self-reported he
        alth and activity lifestyle. Journal of Gerontology: Psychological
        Sciences, 48, P1-P11.
                Examined relationships among health, lifestyle and both information
        processing and intelligence in late life, finding that health and activity
        predicted cognitive performance with the latter being more important.
        Age differences in performance were also minimized when health and
        activity were controlled.

I18     Kausler, D. F. (1990). Motivation, human aging, and cognitive
        performance. Handbook of the psychology of aging (pp. 172-183).
        New York: Academic Press.
                Reviews evidence bearing on the influence of both intrinsic and
        extrinsic motivational factors on cognitive functioning in late life.

I19     Kausler, D. F. (1991). Intelligence. In D. F. Kausler (Ed.),
        Experimental psychology, cognition, and human aging (pp. 660-726).
        New York: Springer-Verlag.
                Excellent discussion of the aging and intelligence literature.
        Includes focus on different theoretical viewpoints, structural change,
        terminal drop, performance vs. competence, intervention and relation-
        ships to other aspects of cognition.

I20     Lachman, M. E., & McArthur, L. Z. (1986). Adulthood age
        differences in causal attributions for cognitive, physical and social
        performance. Psychology and Aging, 1, 127-132.
                When adult attributions for poor performance in several domains by
        aged persons were made, a lack of ability was suggested as an
        explanation. Important paper to the extent that explanations for
        performance may influence subsequent efforts to improve one's skills.

I21     Lachman, M. E., & Leff, R. (1989). Perceived control and intellectual
        functioning in the elderly: A 5-year longitudinal study. Developmental
        Psychology, 25, 722-728.
                Examines changes in control beliefs and intelligence over time as
        well as their antecedents. Focus on the extent to which persons' beliefs

about their intellectual functioning actually predict such performance over time. A unique study with surprising results about the relationships between the two.

I22        Lovelace, E. A. (1990). <u>Aging and cognition: Mental processes, self-awareness, and intervention</u>. Amsterdam: North Holland.

           This edited volume is written to reflect the diversity of growing research efforts in cognitive aging. Special concern is given to individual differences variables and to cognitive interventions with older adults.

I23        Maciel, A. G., Heckhausen, J., & Baltes, P. B. (1994). A life span perspective on the interface between personality and intelligence. In R. J. Sternberg & P. Ruzgis (Eds.), <u>Personality and intelligence</u> (pp. 61-103). Cambridge, MA: Cambridge University Press.

           Taking a lifespan perspective, the relationship between personality and intelligence is explored. Constructs of pluralism and contextualism are emphasized, using wisdom as a prototypical example for discussion.

I24        McGue, M., Hirsch, B., & Lykken, D. T. (1993). Age and the self-perception of ability: A twin study analysis. <u>Psychology and Aging</u>, <u>8</u>, 72-80.

           These authors studied over 1200 monozygotic and dizygotic twin paris aged 27-86 and found little evidence for age or gender effects, suggesting that self concept is formed early in life and that it reflects genetically determined psychological qualities.

I25        Perlmutter, M. (1994). Cognitive skills within the context of adult development and old age. In C. B. Fisher & R. M. Lerner (Eds.), <u>Applied developmental psychology</u> (pp. 101-138). New York: McGraw-Hill.

           Excellent overview of cognition in late life, emphasizing its contextual, everyday components and its impact on the quality of life for the older adult and for society.

I26        Perlmutter, M., & Nyquish, L. (1990). Relationships between self-reported physical and mental health and intelligence performance across adulthood. <u>Journal of Gerontology: Psychological Sciences</u>, <u>45</u>, 145-155.

           Examined relationships among physical health, mental health and intelligence in later life, finding that those who are in poorer physical and mental health perform more poorly on measures of fluid ability.

I27        Salthouse, T. A. (1990). Cognitive competence and expertise in aging. Handbook of the psychology of aging (pp. 311-319). New York: Academic Press.
           Examines the question of why older persons can demonstrate exceptional cognitive performance in the context of a specific environment, despite experiencing declines in other domains of cognitive activity.

I28        Schaie, K. W. (1979). The primary mental abilities in adulthood: An exploration in the development of psychometric intelligence. In P. B. Baltes, D. L. Featherman & R. L. Lerner (Eds.), Life-span development and behavior: V 2 (pp. 68-117).
           Excellent overview of the author's program of research on the development of the primary mental abilities in adulthood. Sets the tone for subsequent research in this area.

I29        Schaie, K. W. (1989). The hazards of cognitive aging. The Gerontologist, 29, 484-493.
           Discusses the application of event history analysis to cognitive decline, enabling one to assess the degree of risk for future cognitive declines. Highlights the role of level of education as a predictor of cognitive change.

I30        Schaie, K. W. (1990). Intellectual development in adulthood. Handbook of the psychology of aging (pp. 291-310). New York: Academic Press.
           Well written, yet compact chapter that emphasizes theoretical and methodological issues in a discussion of age and cohort effects in intelligence, as well as examining practical intelligence and interventions with aged persons.

I31        Schaie, K. W. (1990). Late life potential and cohort differences in mental abilities. In K. W. Schaie (Ed.), Annual review of gerontology and geriatrics: V. 7 (pp. 43-62). New York: Springer.
           Clearly presented description of the author's research on the development of intellectual abilities with attention given to the importance of cohort vs. age as explanations for changes over time in such skills.

I32        Schaie, K. W., & Willis, S. L. (1986). Can decline in adult intellectual functioning be reversed? Developmental Psychology, 22, 223-232.
           This study underscores the impact of cognitive training in late life finding that heuristics instruction on fluid ability skills can return older adults to levels of performance achieved 14 years earlier.

I33     Schaie, K. W., & Willis, S. L. (1993). Age difference patterns of psychometric intelligence in adulthood: Generalizability within and across ability domains. Psychology and Aging, 8, 44-45.
        In an extensive cross-sectional study of over 1500 adults aged 29-88, the authors found more evidence both between and within ability domains for regular age/cohort effects for crystallized than for fluid type skills. Such effects were greater for young vs. older adults than for those at midlife. These findings speak to the degree of generalizability of ability constructs across life stages, important for consistency of measurement of various skills across the life span.

I34     Schaie, K. W., Willis, S. L., Jay, G., & Chipuer, H. (1989). Structural invariance of cognitive abilities across the adult life span: A cross sectional study. Developmental Psychology, 25, 652-662.
        This cross sectional study found evidence for no age-related shifts in the factor loading pattern of abilities, while there were clear age differences in the magnitude of the loadings of specific ability tests on their respective factors important for establishing measurement equivalence.

I35     Schaie, K. W., Willis, S. L., O'Hanlon, A. M. (1994). Perceived intellectual change over seven years. Journal of Gerontology: Psychological Sciences, 49, 108-119.
        Older persons were characterized as optimists, pessimists or realists, depending on the extent to which they accurately predicted seven-year changes in their intellectual performance. In general, perceptions of decline were most common, but varied by gender and by the ability judged.

I36     Schooler, C. (1990). Psychosocial factors and effective cognitive functioning in adulthood. Handbook of the psychology of aging (pp. 347-358). New York: Academic Press.
        Adapts a social psychological approach to cognitive functioning in later life, emphasizing environmental complexity and the role of the environment in influencing adults' values and expectations about their cognitive skills.

I37     Schultz, N. R., Elias, M. F., Robbins, M. A., Streeton, D. H., & Blakeman, N. (1989). A longitudinal study of the performance of hypertensive and hypothensive subjects on the WAIS. Psychology and Aging, 4, 496-503.
        This longitudinal study suggests that untreated hypertension is related to intellectual declines in late life, while for those whose hypertension is treatable, such declines are less severe or even minimal.

I38      Stankov, L. (1988).  Aging, attention, and intelligence.  Psychology
         and Aging, 3, 59-74.
             Examines the unique contribution that attentional processes make in
         accounting for age effects in distinct aspects of intelligence in later life.

I39      Sternberg, R. J. (1990).  Wisdom: Its nature, origins and development.
         Cambridge: Cambridge University Press.
             This edited volume speaks to a relatively new area of research in
         applied cognition.  Thought-provoking examination of wisdom from
         several theoretical perspectives, with several chapters devoted to the
         development of wisdom in both a historical and personal sense.

I40      Sternberg, R. J., & Berg, C. A. (1992).  Intellectual development.
         Cambridge: Cambridge University Press.
             Excellent volume of edited chapters deals with the conceptual and
         empirical aspects of intelligence across the life span with an emphasis
         on adult development.  Included are psychometric, Piagetian, informa-
         tion processing learning theory, sociocultural and contextual approaches
         to intelligence and aging.  A very valuable resource in the area.

I41      Willis, S. L. (1990).  Cognitive training in later adulthood.  Develop-
         mental Psychology, 26, 875-915.
             Series of articles by various authors exploring the many dimensions
         of interventions to improve cognitive performance in later life.
         Includes papers of both an empirical and a theoretical nature.

I42      Willis, S. L., & Schaie, K. W. (1994).  Assessing everyday compe-
         tence in the elderly.  In C. B. Fisher & R. M. Lerner (Eds.), Applied
         developmental psychology (pp. 339-366).  New York: McGraw-Hill
             This chapter explores the role that the assessment of competence
         plays in understanding older adults as well as exploring issues of
         measurement in what is meant by adult competence.

# 7

# *Creativity*

C1    Cohen-Shalev, A. (1989). Old age style: Developmental changes in creative production from a life-span perspective. Journal of Aging Studies, 3, 21-37.

   Reviews creativity research and the use of the biological model of aging to explain the age-related decrement in creativity often cited in the literature. Argues for a life-span developmental approach to the study of creativity and cites recent work by art historians who have introduced the term "Old Age Style" to characterize some of the thematic and formal commonalities appearing with regularity in the works of older painters.

C2    Cole, S. (1979). Age and scientific performance. American Journal of Sociology, 84, 264-272.

   Using cross-sectional and longitudinal designs, the author examined productivity of scientists. The cross-sectional portion of the study showed that over a five year period, the relationship of age to creativity was curvilinear. That is, productivity peaked in the early 40s, leveled off to age 50, and then declined slowly. The longitudinal portion of the study showed, however, that over a 25 year period, the productivity of mathematicians did not change significantly.

C3    Dennis, W. (1966). Creative productivity between the ages of 20 and 80 years. Journal of Gerontology, 21, 1-8.

   As Lehmans primary critic, Dennis enumerates the weaknesses of the methodology used in Age and achievement. This paper summarizes those flaws, such as the method by which Lehman gathered his data and the conclusions he made based on a cross-sectional investigation of those data, rather than a comprehensive examination of the life spans of his subjects. Dennis also provides an alternative to Lehman's work by examining creative achievements of those over the age of 79. He reports wide variability in individuals as well as within fields of creativity.

C4      Horner, K. L., Rushton, J. P., & Vernon, P. A. (1986). Relation between aging and research productivity of academic psychologists. Psychology and Aging, 1, 319-324.
        Examined research productivity among 1000 academic psychologists. Although the general trend showed a peak in the early 40s followed by a gradual decline, researchers who were strong publishers initially tended to remain prolific.

C5      Lehman, H. C. (1953). Age and achievement. Philadelphia: American Philosophical Society.
        This much criticized work was the starting point for a new field of gerontological study. Lehman describes his large-scale investigation into the course of creativity throughout the life span. Using a cross-sectional design, he examined the ages at which notable scholars, politicians, heads of business, scientists, and artists made their most significant contributions. He concluded that creativity declined strikingly after age 40. His work has been widely refuted, but still remains as an interesting part of history in the field.

C6      Pruyser, P. W. (1987). Creativity in aging persons. Bulletin of the Menninger Clinic, 51, 425-435.
        Discusses aging as a creative process within the view that old-age has specific differences from previous life stages. Asserts that maturation provides unique opportunity to express creativity.

C7      Pufal-Struzic, I. (1992). Differences in personality and self-knowledge of creative persons at different ages: A comparative analysis. Special Issue: Geragogics: European research in gerontological education and educational gerontology. Gerontology and Geriatrics Education, 13, 71-90.
        Examined value system priorities, self-knowledge and the role of creativity, motivation of creativity, and psychological needs of 177 painters, poets, writers, and film directors aged 20-87 years, as well as 105 non-creator controls. Older creators tended to value their work more and have higher levels of self-assessment based on experience and creative output. Creators showed greater self-sufficiency, independence, and resistance to adversity than non-creators, despite intense neurotic tendencies that did not interfere with work.

C8      Reif, F. & Strauss, A. (1965). The impact of rapid discovery upon
        the scientist's career. Social Problems, 12, 299-311.
            This classic paper explains how scientists may become obscure due
        the rapid accumulation of new scientific knowledge, especially in the
        social sciences. The authors suggest two alternatives for the scientist--
        changing areas or going into nonresearch careers. Changing areas re-
        quires reeducation and creativity, whereas moving into nonresearch
        careers relieves much of the pressure to be creative and productive.

C9      Shearring, H. A. (1992). Creativity and older adults. Leadership and
        Organization Development Journal, 13, 11-16.
            Argues that creativity is a function of the Three R's: recognizing
        problems and opportunities, retrieving relevant material from memory,
        and rearranging this material to form new patterns. Also argues that
        these skills can be taught, regardless of age. Presents a basic syllabus
        for a creativity development plan for older adults.

C10     Simonton, D. K. (1975). Age and literary creativity: A cross-cultural
        and transhistorical survey. Journal of Cross-Cultural Psychology, 6,
        259-277.
            Examined the course of creativity in the fields of poetry, informa-
        tive prose, and imaginative prose over the life span and across cultures.
        This extensive investigation revealed differential creative peaks for the
        three types of literature, with poetry peaking earliest and informative
        prose peaking latest. These peaks were uniform across cultures.
        Simonton explains these trends within the context of language as well
        as emotional development over the life span.

C11     Simonton, D. K. (1977). Eminence, creativity, and geographic
        marginality: A recursive structural equation model. Journal of
        Personality and Social Psychology, 35, 805-816.
            Investigated the productivity of ten eminent composers of classical
        music by examining the ratio of major works to total works during
        five-year intervals. Results indicate that creative productivity remains
        stable over the life span, with a slight peak during the early 30s.

C12     Simonton, D. K. (1989). Age and creative productivity: Nonlinear
        estimation on an information-processing model. International Journal
        of Aging and Human Development, 29, 23-37.
            Describes a two-step cognitive model that explains the relationship
        between age and creativity. Two information-processing parameters,
        the ideation and elaboration rates, are give as a mathematical function
        describing the age curve and its variability across disciplines. The

author validates the model by applying it to several of his previously published works.

C13     Simonton, D. K. (1990). Creativity and wisdom in aging. Handbook of the psychology of aging (pp. 320-329). New York: Academic Press.
        Well written presentation of the nature and determinants of creativity and wisdom in later life. Presents a variety of perspectives on creativity; well referenced.

C14     Simonton, D. K. (1990). Does creativity decline in the later years? Definition, data, and theory. In M. Perlmutter (Ed.), Late life potential (pp. 83-112). Washington, DC: Gerontological Society of America.
        Well-written chapter exploring the nature of creativity, theories of creative productivity, and the effect of age on creative achievements.

C15     Simonton, D. K. (1991). Creative productivity throughout the adult years. Generations, 15, 13-16.
        Describes the generalized age curve as a function of career rather than chronological age. Although the author states that the rate of output in the 70s falls to about 50% of the rate observed at the career optimum in the 30s and 40s, age curves vary significantly across disciplines. Additionally, substantial individual plasticity is observed, and older adults often experience a creative renaissance in their final years.

C16     Simonton, D. K. (1991). Emergence and realization of genius: The lives and works of 120 classical composers. Journal of Personality and Social Psychology, 61, 829-840.
        Examined the preparatory phases and individual differences in the creative lives of 120 classical composers from the Renaissance to the 20th century. Productivity variables were rated for both themes and works, and examined with regard to their relationships to eminence, lifetime output, maximum annual output, and ages of first lessons, first composition, first hit, best hit, last hit, and death. Questions are raised as to the early childhood roots of creativity.

C17     Simonton, D. K. (1990). Creativity in the later years: Optimistic prospects for achievement. The Gerontologist, 30, 626-631.
        Outlines considerations that suggest that decline in productivity in the final years of life is not imminent: the actual magnitude of the age decrement, the role of extrinsic influences, the contigency on career

age, the impact of individual differences in creative potential, and the interdisciplinary variation in the age curves.

C18     Smith, G. J., & Van-der-Meer, G. (1990). Creativity in old age. Creativity Research Journal, 3, 249-264.

In an examination of how older adults (aged 67-86 yrs) experience illness, aging, and death, measurements of anxiety, self-image, and creativity were administered. Results showed that creative subjects viewed life more positively, had a less defensive attitude toward illness, were more flexible and emotional in their self-projections.

C19     Zuckerman, H., & Merton, R. K. (1972). Age, aging and age structure in science. In M. Riley, M. Johnson, & A. Foner (Eds.), Aging and society: Vol. 3. A sociology of age stratification (pp. 14-42). New York: Russell Sage Foundation.

These authors explain why codifiability, or scientific rigor, impacts the age at which scientists tend to make important discoveries. In highly codified fields, creativity at a younger age is favored, due to the compact body of knowledge which is more easily gained by young scientists, as well as a larger consensus of scientists working on a single problem.

# 8

# *Interpersonal Relationships*

IP1     Albert, S. M. (1991). Cognition of caregiving tasks: Multidimensional scaling of the caregiver task domain. The Gerontologist, 31, 726-734.
        Interesting paper reporting the identification of distinct dimensions of the caregiving experience useful for both research and counseling-related purposes.

IP2     Antonucci, T. C. (1990). Social supports and social relationships. In R. Binstock, E. Shanas, & L. George (Eds.), Handbook of aging and the social sciences (pp. 205-226). New York: Academic Press.
        This chapter examines the construct of social support incorporating the notion of the convoy in examining social relationships in later life. Examines sex differences in social support, family support, and friendships as well as their implications for the health of older persons.

IP3     Barer, B. M., & Johnson, C. L. (1990). A critique of the caregiving literature. The Gerontologist, 30, 26-29.
        Critically examines the literature on caregiving in terms of both conceptual and especially empirical issues. Brief, yet valuable paper.

IP4     Barnes-Farrell, J. L., & Piotrowski, M. (1989). Workers' perceptions of the discrepencies between chronological age and personal age; You're only as young as you feel. Psychology and Aging, 4, 376-377.
        Explored persons feelings about their personal age relative to their actual age, finding that most felt younger than they really were. The proportion of those feeling younger increased with greater age, while the opposite occurred for those who were younger.

IP5        Bengtson, V., Rosenthal, C., & Burton, L. (1990). Families and
           aging: Diversity and heterogeneity. In R. Binstock, E. Shanas & L.
           George (Eds.), Handbook of aging and the social sciences (pp. 263-
           287). New York: Academic Press.
                Examines the evolving nature of the family in later life, stressing the
           breadth of how families need to be defined. Intergenerational
           relationships, marriage, grandparenting, sibling relationships and
           widowhood are discussed. Excellent resource.

IP6        Bretschneider, J., & McCoy, N. (1988). Sexual interest and behavior
           in 80 to 102 year olds. Archieves of Sexual Behavior, 17, 109-129.
                Details both sexual interest and sexual behavior, noting the
           increasing discrepancy between the two by age and sex.

IP7        Burton, L. (1993). Families and aging. Amityville, NY: Baywood.
                This edited volume deals with many dimensions of today's changing
           family as it relates to aging. Issues of definition, demography, divorce,
           remarriage, ethnicity, grandparenting, sibling relations, and caregiving
           are discussed. Includes contemporary bibliography.

IP8        Cantor, M. F. (1991). Family and community: Changing roles in an
           aging society. The Gerontologist, 31, 337-346.
                A model is presented wherein the family and formal help sources
           are interrelated in providing care for frail elderly.

IP9        Carter, B., & McGoldrick, M. (1988). Overview: The changing
           family life cycle - a framework for family therapy. In B. Carter & M.
           McGoldrick (Eds.), The changing family life cycle: A framework for
           family therapy (pp. 1-25). Boston: Allyn & Bacon.
                Describes a modified family life cycle approach to family develop-
           ment, incorporating a systems approach to understanding the nature of
           the transition to the "family of later life."

IP10       Caspi, A., Bem, D., & Elder, G. (1989). Continuities and conse-
           quences of interactional styles across the life course. Journal of
           Personality, 57, 375-406.
                Found that among men, there was consistency in the personality
           patterns across time, despite changes in levels of specific behaviors.
           Interesting discussion of the consequences of early interactional styles
           on later adult development.

IP11       Carstensen, L. (1992). Social and emotional patterns in adulthood:
           Support for socioemotional selectivity theory. Psychology and Aging,
           7, 331-338.

Interviews conducted longitudinally for 50 men and women over a 30 year time span indicate a decline in interactions with friends and acquaintances with a concommitant increase in interactions with spouses and siblings.

IP12  Cherlin, A. C., & Furstenberg, F. (1986). The new American grandparent. New York: Basic Books.
Within the context of an overview of grandparenting, presents a new typology of grandparental styles: Companionate, remote and involved. In some ways these styles resemble others that have preceeded them. Excellent resource on grandparenting.

IP13  Cicirelli, V. G., & Nussbaum, J. F. (1989). Relationships with siblings in later life. In J. F. Nussbaum (Ed.), Life-span communication: Normative processes (pp. 283-301). Hillsdale, NJ: Lawrence Erlbaum.
Excellent overview of sibling relationships in later life. In light of the role that siblings play in defining the convoy, this chapter is quite important.

IP14  Connidis, I. A., & Davies, L. (1990). Confidants and companions in later life: The place of family and friends. Journal of Gerontology: Social Sciences, 45, 151-159.
Speaks to the importance of the convoy of social support in examining the role of family vs. friends as confidants.

IP15  Crockett, W. H., & Hummert, M. L. (1987). Perceptions of aging and the elderly. In K. W. Schaie (Ed.), Annual review of gerontology and geriatrics: V. 7 (pp. 217-242). New York: Springer.
Excellent historical review of myths and stereotypical beliefs about older adults and aging as well as the basis for such beliefs.

IP16  Datan, N., Greene, A. L., & Reese, H. W. (1986). Life-span developmental psychology: Intergenerational relations. Hillsdale, NJ: Lawrence Erlbaum.
This edited volume deals with a variety of conceptual and methodological dimensions of research on intergenerational relationships. With respect to aging, specific chapters deal with elder abuse and caregiving, multigenerational change and family influences on intellectual functioning.

IP17  Gatz, M., Bengtson, V. L., & Blum, M. J. (1990). Caregiving families. Handbook of the psychology of aging (pp. 405-426). New York: Academic Press.

Well researched review of caregiving in later life from a family perspective, with the presentation of a model for understanding caregiver stress and coping.

IP18    Gentry, M., & Shulman, A. D. (1988). Remarriage as a coping response for widowhood. Psychology and Aging, 3, 191-196.
Examines the consequences of remarriage after widowhood, finding that they can be quite adaptive for some elderly adults to help them cope with depression, loss, and social isolation.

IP19    Heckhausen, J., & Krueger, J. (1993). Developmental expectations for the self and most other people: Age grading in three functions of social comparison. Developmental Psychology, 29, 539-548.
Interesting study which identified 3 models of social comparison (self vs. others) individuals of varying ages use in formulating beliefs about development.

IP20    Hill, R., & Mattessich, P. (1979). Family development theory and life-span development. In P. B. Baltes, D. L. Featherman & R. L. Lerner (Eds.), Life-span development and behavior: V 2 (pp. 162-204).
A novel life cycle approach to the family's development from a systems perspective, emphasizing multiple levels of understanding of the family.

IP21    Hummert, M. L. (1990). Multiple stereotypes of elderly and young adults: A comparison of structures and evaluation. Psychology and Aging, 5, 182-193.
Created a complex stereotypical picture of perceptions of younger versus older adults. While equally inaccurate, both younger and older persons were perceived both negatively and positively by adults of varying age.

IP22    Kahn, R. L., & Antonucci, T. (1980). Convoys over the life course: Attachment, roles, and social support. In P. B. Baltes, D. L. Featherman & R. L. Lerner (Eds.), Life-span development and behavior: V 3 (pp. 254-286). New York: Academic Press.
Seminal chapter on the definition and development of the convoy of social support. It also discusses the measurement aspects of the construct of social support.

IP23    Knight, B. G., Lutzky, S. M., & Macofsky-Urban, F. (1993). A meta-analytic review of interventions for caregiver distress: Recommendations for future research. The Gerontologist, 33, 240-248.

A decade's worth of research is reviewed, suggesting that while individual interventions and respite are moderately effective, group interventions are less so. Well integrated in its discussion of research issues.

IP24    Lawton, M. P., Kleban, M. H., Moss, M., Rovine, M., & Glicksman, A. (1989). Measuring caregiving appraisal. Journal of Gerontology: Psychological Sciences, 44, 61-71.

Reports on the development of a multi-faceted instrument to assess caregivers evaluation and perception of the experience of caring for an aged or impaired family member. Includes each subscale's items in an appendix.

IP25    Levenson, R. W., Carstensen, L. L., & Gottman, J. M. (1993). Long-term marriage: Age, gender, and satisfaction. Psychology and Aging, 8, 301-313.

In this cross sectional study, older marriages were viewed positively, and characterized by reduced conflict, equivalent levels of physical and mental health and few gender differences in sources of pleasure.

IP26    Levitt, M. J., Weber, R. A., & Guacci, N. (1993). Convoys of social support: An intergenerational analysis. Psychology and Aging, 8, 323-326.

Attempts to empirically define the convoy across the adult life span using a cultural diverse sample. While many of the convoy's structural characteristics e.g., size, degree of support, were constant across age, the balance of friends vs. family differentiated persons by age.

IP27    Pearlin, L. I., Mullan, J. T., Semple, S. J., & Skaff, M. M. (1990). Caregiving and the stress process: An overview of concepts and their measures. The Gerontologist, 30, 583-594.

Presents an overview of caregiving and stress as well as a model explicating their relationship with an emphasis on measurement.

IP28    Pruchno, R., & Kleban, M. H. (1993). Caring for an institutionalized parent: The role of coping strategies. Psychology and Aging, 8, 18-25.

In studying how adult children deal with their parents institutionalization, the authors found that emotion-focused coping strategies mediate the relationship between stress and mental health. This suggests that different coping skills may be more or less important in helping one deal with a parent who is a nursing home resident.

IP29    Roberts, K. A., & Scott, J. P. (1986).  Friendships of older men and
        women: Exchange patterns and satisfaction.  Psychology and Aging, 1,
        103-109.
            This study reinforces the importance of distinguishing between deep
        and interested related friendships in late life as a function of perceived
        equity.  It suggests that intimacy needs may be defined differently for
        old men and women, incorporating gender differences in the perception
        of equity in relationships.

IP30    Ryff, C. (1989).  In the eye of the beholder: Views of psychological
        well-being among middle aged and older adults.  Psychology and
        Aging, 4, 195-210.
            Explored adults' perceptions of maturity, finding that persons who
        were "other-oriented" were most likely to be described as mature
        irrespective of the age of the perceiver.  In contrast, perceptions of
        aging varied by age and by when such changes were negative or
        positive in nature.

IP31    Seltzer, M. M., & Ryff, C. D. (1994).  Parenting across the life span:
        Normative and nonnormative cases.  In D. L. Featherman, R. M.
        Lerner & M. Perlmutter (Eds.), Life-span development and behavior:
        V. 12 (pp. 1-41).  Hillsdale, NJ: Lawrence Erlbaum.
            Examines the parent role across the life span with attention to the
        regularity of the circumstances under which one becomes a parent.

IP32    Shore, R. J., & Hayslip, B. (1994).  Custodial grandparenting:
        Implications for children's development.  In A. K. Gottfried & A. W.
        Gottfried (Eds.), Redefining families: Implications for children's
        development (pp. 171-220).  New York: Plenum.
            Reviews the literature on grandparenting as well as presenting and
        testing a model describing the determinants of multiple indicators of
        well-being in a sample of 200 custodial and traditional grandparents.

IP33    Smith, G. C., Smith, M. F., & Toseland, R. W. (1991).  Problems
        identified by family caregivers in counseling.  The Gerontologist, 31,
        15-22.
            Excellent paper discussing the stresses and strains of family
        caregiving with the context of counseling.  This article contains a
        content analysis of the problems that caregiver daughters and daughters-
        in-law elected to work on during counseling.  Analysis yielded seven
        categories including improving coping skills, meeting elder's card
        needs, responding to family issues, concern over the caregiver-recipient
        relationship, eliciting formal and informal supports, feelings of

inadequacy and guilt, and planning for elder's future. Case examples illustrate problems, and the authors discuss practice implications.

IP34    Smith, G. C., Smith, M. F., & Toseland, R. W. (1991). Problems identified by family caregivers in counseling. The Gerontologist, 31, 15-22.

This article contains a content analysis of the problems that caregiver daughters and daughters-in-law elected to work on during counseling. Analysis yielded seven categories including improving coping skills, meeting elder's card needs, responding to family issues, concern over the caregiver-recipient relationship, eliciting formal and informal supports, feelings of inadequacy and guilt, and planning for elder's future. Case examples illustrate problems, and the authors discuss practice implications.

IP35    Stoller, E. P., & Gibson, R. C. (1994). Worlds of difference: Inequality in the aging experience. Thousand Oaks, CA: Pine Forge Press.

This collection of articles examines the psychosocial facets of disadvantage and priviledge in later life based on gender, race, or class. Most entries have a very positive tone to them, though many are soberingly negative. Very interesting and insightful reading, specific sections focus on productivity, the family and health and mortality.

IP36    Thomas, J. L. (1986). Gender differences in satisfaction with grandparenting. Psychology and Aging, 1, 215-219.

Extends what we know about grandparenting to both men and women, incorporating factors such as gender, age and health of the grandparent. Women expressed more satisfaction than did men, who were most satisfied if they were older and actively involved in child rearing.

IP37    Toseland, R. W., & Zarit, S. H. (1989). Symposium: Effectiveness of caregiver groups. The Gerontologist, 29, 437-483.

Excellent series of articles examining the rationale for and effectiveness of caregiver support groups. While some papers are conceptual, others are empirical in nature.

IP38    Whitlatch, C. J., Zarit, S. H., & VonEye, A. (1991). Efficacy of interventions with caregivers: A reanalysis. The Gerontologist, 31, 9-14.

A novel study which highlights the role that even brief family counseling can play in helping caregivers deal with their burdens, using prediction analysis as a method of data evaluation.

IP39    Zarit, S. H., & Reid, J. D. (1994). Family caregiving and the older
        family.  In C. B. Fisher & R. M. Lerner (Eds.), <u>Applied developmen-</u>
        <u>tal psychology</u> (pp. 237-264).  New York: McGraw-Hill.
             This well written chapter examines the challenges of family
        caregiving in late life, emphasizing its impact on individuals as well as
        on the social and political context which determines the resources from
        which older caregivers and care recipients can draw.

# 9

# *Mental Health and Psychopathology*

MH1   Addonizio, G., & Alexopoulos, G. S. (1993). Affective disorders in the elderly. International Journal of Geriatric Psychiatry, 8, 41-47.

This review article discusses the clinical data and research in affective disorders such as dementia, depression, and bipolar disorder in the elderly. Epidemiology, diagnosis, treatment, course of illness, biological markers, and pathophysiology are topics also discussed.

MH2   Alexopoulos, G. S., Young, R. C., & Abrams, R. C. (1989). Chronicity and relapse in geriatric depression. Biological Psychiatry, 26, 551-564.

This article offers a review of the literature on predictors of chronicity of depression and relapse among the elderly. It describes specific predictors in each case.

MH3   Almeida, O. P., Howard, R., Forstl, H., & Levy, R. (1992). Late paraphrenia: A review. International Journal of Geriatric Psychiatry, 7, 543-548.

This article reviews the literature on delusional-hallucinatory disorders of elderly persons. The authors also provide evidence that they suggest points to a premature decision to throw out the concept of late paraphrenia. It is argued that the processes underlying late PRP differ from those underlying schizophrenia and other late-onset delusional disorders.

MH4   Alzheimer, A. (1991). On certain peculiar diseases of old age. History of Psychiatry, 2, 74-101.

This article presents A. Alzheimer's (1911) description of the clinical and neuropathological features of Alzheimer's disease (AD) followed by a review of the current literature. In this way the unresolved problems which have surfaced since Alzheimer's first paper are discussed.

MH5    Aries, T. (Ed.). (1992). Recent advances in psychogeriatrics-Number 2. Edinburgh: Churchill Livingstone.
       This volume includes work that concentrates on recent developments and advances in the field of psychogeriatrics. Works included focus on the biological understanding of diseases, epidemiology, clinical aspects of functional disorders, service development and also caregiver needs and user involvement.

MH6    Barsky, A. J. (1993). The diagnosis and management of hypochondriacal concerns in the elderly. Journal of Geriatric Psychiatry, 26, 129-141.
       The author addresses both the specific diagnosable psychiatric disorder, and the nonspecific symptom of hypochondriasis as they relate to aging. In addition he offers information about the management of hypochondriasis as it occurs in the elderly.

MH7    Basal, M. E. (Ed.). (1994). Depression in the elderly: Clinical considerations and therapeutic approaches [Special Issue]. International Journal of Experimental and Clinical Gerontology, 40 (1).
       This special issue contains works on the epidemiology, management, and clinical presentation of depression in the elderly. The use and risks of antidepressants is also included as a topic.

MH8    Bienenfeld, D. (Ed.). (1990). Verwoerdt's clinical geropsychiatry (3rd ed.). Baltimore: Williams & Wilkins.
       This text is designed to be helpful for general psychiatrists, residents, fellows, and primary care physicians, assisting in diagnosis, assessment, and care of older adults. It contains chapters on many of disorders as well as on the physical changes with age, aging and the central nervous system, psychiatry in the nursing home, etc.

MH9    Birren, J. E., Sloane, R. B., & Cohen, G. D. (Eds.). (1992). Handbook of mental health and aging. San Diego, CA: Academic.
       This comprehensive volume is the premiere reference in the field. The chapters it contains are written by prominent researchers in the epidemiology of mental disorders, mood disorders and suicide, anxiety, personality disorders, schizophrenia, Alzheimer's Disease, alcohol and substance-use disorders, sleep disorders, and developmental disabilities.

Includes a series of chapters on a variety of assessment techniques and modes of therapy, as well as chapters on nursing home care, forensics, and the economics of mental health care. Concluding chapter is integrative in nature. Well referenced.

MH10 Blazer, D. (1989). Depression in late life: An update. In M. P. Lawton (Ed.), Annual review of gerontology and geriatrics, Vol. 9 (pp. 197-231). New York: Springer.

The author of this chapter offers a review of the recent advances in the clinical investigation of depression. Research in the areas of the epidemiology of depression in later life, the psychobiology of late-life depression, and the recent advances in the treatment of depression are included.

MH11 Blazer, D. (1990). Emotional problems in later life. New York: Springer.

Excellent presentation of the mental/emotional disorders of later life. Especially valuable are the case examples.

MH12 Bolla-Wilson, K., & Bleeker, M. L. (1989). Absence of depression in elderly adults. Journal of Gerontology: Psychological Sciences, 44, 53-55.

Older persons reported more somatic depressive symptoms than did the young, skewing data suggesting an increasing prevalence of depression with age. Recommendations for assessment are made.

MH13 Brink, T. L. (1986). Clinical gerontology: A guide to assessment and intervention. New York: Haworth Press.

Excellent collection of chapters dealing with assessment and psychotherapy as they relate to older adults. Specific chapters deal with for example, neuropsychological assessment, projective testing, depression, anxiety, individual therapy, family approaches, pain management and suicide. Though somewhat dated, it is nevertheless a valuable resource.

MH14 Brink, T. L. (1990). Mental health in the nursing home. New York: Haworth Press.

This reprinted volume of the Clinical Gerontologist consists of chapters addressing the adjustment of families and older persons to nursing home placement as well as varieties of group therapy with aged residents.

MH15 Brink, T. R. (Ed.). The clinical gerontologist. Binghamton, NY: Haworth Press.

Specialty journal devoted to clinical gerontological practice. Includes both case study and empirically based articles.

MH16    Burvill, P. W., Stampfer, H., & Hall, W. (1986). Does depressive illness in the elderly have a poorer prognosis? Australian and New Zealand Journal of Psychiatry, 20, 422-427.

This article reviews longitudinal studies concerning risk and prognostic factors of depressive illness in the elderly. The authors discuss research on a variety of possible prognostic factors such as physical illness, severity of depression, and social factors, etc.

MH17    Butler, R. N., Lewis, M., & Sunderland, T. (1991). Aging and mental health: Positive psychosocial and biomedical approaches. New York: Macmillan.

The fourth edition of this standard reference discusses aging in general as well as both functional and organic mental disorders. Specific chapters deal with evaluation, home care, institutional care and therapies.

MH18    Byre, E. J., Smith, C. W., & Arie, T. (1991). The diagnosis of dementia: I. Clinical and pathological criteria: A review of the literature. International Journal of Geriatric Psychiatry, 6, 199-208.

This article looks at the theoretical basis for the diagnosis of dementia and discusses three definitions of Alzheimer's disease. The complexity of the diagnosis is addressed.

MH19    Carstensen, L. L., & Edelstein, B. A. (1987). Handbook of clinical gerontology. New York: Pergamon Press.

Comprehensive, though somewhat dated volume dealing with both normal and pathological aging. Specific sections devoted to psychiatric, medical and behavioral problems. Includes a section on social issues.

MH20    Cohen, G. D. (1990). Psychopathology and mental health in the mature and elderly adult. In J. E. Birren, & K. W. Schaie (Eds.), Handbook of the psychology of aging (pp. 359-371). San Diego: Academic Press.

The author addresses the difficulty in recognizing mental disorders in the aged, including the distinction between normal aging and disorder. In addition discussion includes issues of epidemiology of mental disorders and the interaction between mental and physical disorders for older persons. Possible symptomology signaling mental disorder is also presented.

MH21   Cusford, P. A., & Arnold, E. (1992). Eating disorders in later life: A review. International Journal of Geriatric Psychiatry, 7, 491-498.
This article reviews the literature on anorexia nervosa and bulimia nervosa among older adults. Most of the works reviewed suggest that older adults have classical features of the disorders similar to their younger counterparts. The complexity of the etiology of eating disorders in the elderly is also discussed.

MH22   Decarli, C., Kaye, J. A., Horwitz, B., & Rapoport, S. I. (1990). Critical analysis of the use of computer-assisted transverse axial tomography to study human brain in aging and dementia of the Alzheimer type. Neurology, 40, 872-883.
This article reviews the literature on the use of computerized tomography (CT) for the diagnosis of Alzheimer's Disease. According the works reviewed, CT is a helpful tool for studying the older brain and the brain of persons with AD and is most effective when used longitudinally.

MH23   Fisher, F. E., Zeiss, A. M., & Carstensen, L. L. (1993). Psychopathology in the aged. In P. B. Sutker, & H. E. Adams (Eds.), Comprehensive handbook of psychopathology (2nd ed.) (pp. 815-842). New York: Plenum.
This chapter is designed to examine the theoretical assumptions and empirical status of research on psychopathology in old age. The methodological problems of confounding age and cohort effects and the lack of standardized measures normed on the older persons are discussed.

MH24   Deimling, G. T., & Bass, D. M. (1986). Symptoms of mental impairment among elderly adults and their effects on family caregivers. Journal of Gerontology, 41, 778-784.
This study explores the relative disruptive effects on caregivers' mental health of a number of diverse symptoms of dementia. Interesting findings with clear practical implications.

MH25   Feil, N. (1993). The validation breakthrough. Baltimore: Health Professions Press.
Provocative book examining the assumptions and techniques of validation therapy with impaired elders. Well written, it is full of case examples.

MH26   Foster, J. M., & Gallagher, D. (1986). An exploratory study comparing depressed and nondepressed elders' coping strategies. Journal of Gerontology, 41, 91-93.

Equal sample size groups of depressed/nondepressed elders were given a self-report coping behavior measure that asked them to identify strategies used in response to (a) a recent major life event, and (b) the experience of "feeling down", or "depressed." The depressed group reported a greater use of avoidance coping behavior than did the nondepressed sample and they were also more likely to use emotional discharge as a coping technique. The nondepressed sample rated all methods of coping as more helpful than did the depressed sample.

MH27   Gatz, M., & Pearson, C. G. (1988).  Ageism revised and the provision of psychological services.  American Psychologist, 43, 189-194.
Reevaluates the quality of psychological services offered to older adults in light of recently held misperceptions about normal and abnormal aging as well as intervention.

MH28   Gatz, M., & Smyer, M. A. (1992).  The mental health system and older adults in the 1990's.  American Psychologist, 47, 741-751.
This broad based article reviews mental health services for older adults over the last decade as a means of predicting salient issues for such persons in the 1990's.

MH29   Giancola, P. R., & Zeichmer, A. (1993).  Aggressive behavior in the elderly: A critical review. Clinical Gerontologist, 13, 3-22.
This review article contains discussion of the parameters and prevalence of aggressive behavior in the elderly.  Issues of etiology and treatment are also addressed.

MH30   Gray, G. R., & Hayslip, B. (1990). Drug use and abuse among older adults and their implications for practitioners. The Southwestern, 3, 33-52.
A number of issues pertaining to drug use and abuse among aged persons are discussed.  The authors focus on the physiological factors, definition of use and abuse, and the implications of accurate assessment of drug and alcohol abuse among older adults. The complexity of the issue is stressed.

MH31   Helmchen, H., & Linden, M. (1993). The differentiation between depression and dementia in the very old. Ageing and Society, 13, 589-617.
This study provides findings from the Berlin Aging Study which permitted analysis on data from a heterogenous and primarily non-clinical community population. The results indicate that depression and dementia exhibit distinctive psychopathological features, but that dementia may mask depressive symptoms.

MH32   Heston, L. L., & White, J. A. (1991). <u>The vanishing mind: A</u>
<u>practical guide to Alzheimer's Disease and other dementias</u>. New
York: W. H. Freeman.
   Down to earth, readable discussion of all types of dementia to
include options for treatment and care as well as the financial and
interpersonal aspects of dementing illness. Well written.

MH33   <u>International Journal of Geriatric Psychiatry</u>, Special Issue: Affective
disorders in old age. V. 6, 1991.
   This issue presents information concerning a variety of affective
disorders in old age. The following issues are discussed: outcome,
etiology and symptoms of affective disorders in old age, suicide in the
elderly, neuroanatomical and neurochemical changes in elderly affective
disorders, and depressive pseudodementia.

MH34   Kemp, B. J., & Mitchell, J. (1992). Functional assessment in geriatric
mental health. In J. E. Birren, R. B. Sloane, & G. D. Cohen (Eds.),
<u>Handbook of mental health and aging</u> (pp. 672-698). New York:
Academic Press.
   Presents an overview of geriatric assessment using a hierarchy of
levels of competence approach to organizing and discussing the
objectives and methods of clinical functional geriatric assessment
procedures.

MH35   Koenig, H. G., & Blazer (1992). Mood disorders and suicide. In J. E.
Birren, R. B. Sloane, & G. D. Cohen   (Eds.), <u>Handbook of mental</u>
<u>health and aging</u> (pp. 379-410). San Diego: Academic Press.
   This chapter offers a comprehensive and authoritative review of
relevant research and critical issues in the areas of mood disorders and
suicide. Contains valuable information on epidemiology and differential diagnosis as well as patient management.

MH36   Kruessler, D. (1990). Personality disorder in the elderly. <u>Hospital and</u>
<u>Community Psychiatry</u>, <u>41</u>, 1325-1329.
   This review article focuses on the literature on personality disorders
(PDs) among older adults. The author suggests that Pds among the
elderly are best understood in behavioral terms and therefore may be
masked in the elderly by certain age-related behavioral changes. The
author argues for age-associated criteria.

MH37   Lacro, J. P., Harris, M. J., & Jeste, D. V. (1993). Late life psychosis.
<u>International Journal of Geriatric Psychiatry</u>, <u>8</u>, 49-57.
   The authors of this article present a brief review of the results of
recent research in late life psychosis (LLP). Their discussion includes

the topics of late onset schizophrenia, older patients with early onset schizophrenia, delusional disorder, psychosis in patients with dementia, psychosis in patients with depression, and miscellaneous psychoses.

MH38   Lamberty, G. J., & Bieliauskas, L. A. (1993). Distinguishing between depression and dementia in the elderly: A review of neuropsychological findings. Archives of Clinical Neuropsychology, 8, 149-170.

The authors have centered their literature review on recent neuropsychological studies comparing normal elderly, depressed patients, and patients with progressive dementias. It appears that neuropsychological assessment is helpful in distinguishing between depression and dementia. The authors present a descriptive scheme for categorizing elderly and suggest that the use of the term pseudodementia end.

MH39   LaRue, A. (1992). Aging and neuropsychological assessment. New York: Plenum.

First rate reference on the neuropsychology of aging. Specific chapters deal with the aging brain, cognitive aging, neuropsychological assessment, the dementias and depression. Examples of both normal and pathological performance are provided.

MH40   Leibowitz, B., & Niederche, G. (1992). Concepts and issues in mental health and aging. In J. E. Birren, R. B. Sloane, & G. D. Cohen (Eds.), Handbook of mental health and aging (pp. 3-25). New York: Academic Press.

Excellent discussion of concepts and issues in mental health and aging. Strong research base in examining salient concerns in mental health and mental health care delivery.

MH41   Lewinsohn, P. M., Rohde, P., Seeley, J. R., & Fischer, S. A. (1991). Age and depression: Unique and shared effects. Psychology and Aging, 6, 247-260.

This excellent article discusses those components of depression that differentiate young and older adults. Valuable in differential diagnoses.

MH42   Light, E., & Lebowitz, B. D. (1989). Alzheimer's disease treatment and family stress: Directions for research. Rockville, MD: MINH.

Comprehensive edited volume is very research oriented in its examination of Alzheimer's Disease and caregiver stress. While each chapter is very specific in content, they are well-written. Excellent reviews of the literature in an area of growing importance.

MH43    Maiden, R. J. (1987). Learned helplessness and depression: A test of the reformulated model. Journal of Gerontology, 42, 60-64.

This article compared the old model of learned helplessness with the new reformulated one. Fifty elderly depressed/nondepressed women were given a guessing task which they believed was non-random but was actually based on a table of random numbers. The depressed women attributed failure to lack of ability and success to luck, while the nondepressed women attributed failure to bad luck and success to high ability.

MH44    Miller, M. (1979). Suicide after 60: The final alternative: New York: Springer.

Classic study of older male suicide based on interviews with bereaved family members and spouses. Includes a section on research with older suicides.

MH45    Miller, N. E., & Cohen, G. D. (Eds.). (1987). Schizophrenia and aging: Schizophrenia, paranoia, and schizophreniform disorders in later life. New York: Guilford.

This book covers phenomenology, epidemiology, clinical course, treatment and outcome of both early and late onset schizophrenia. It focuses on individuals with an early diagnosis of schizophrenia who are followed into old age and those individuals who received the diagnosis only it later life. Much attention is given to the differences between early and late onset forms of the disorder.

MH46    Mui, A. C. (1993). Self-reported depressive symptoms among black and hispanic elders: A sociocultural perspective. Journal of Applied Gerontology, 12, 170-187.

The author offers information from a study which examined depressive symptoms and the sources of depressive symptoms among black and hispanic frail elders. The overall results indicated that women reported more depressive symptoms and some of the common predictors were being female, greater numbers of physical illness, poor perceived health, more perceived unmet needs, and less sense of control in life.

MH47    Murley, J. E., & Silver, A. J. (1988). Anorexia in the elderly. Neurobiology of Aging, 9, 9-16.

The authors present a review of current literature and suggest that weight loss and anorexia occur commonly in the elderly. According to the studies reviewed, in many cases the anorexia can be attributed to associated disease processes. However, it does seem that true anorexia does occur in older adults.

MH48   National Institute of Health (1991).  Diagnosis and treatment of depression in late life: Consensus statement.  Bethesda, MD: NIH.
       Public-service oriented report of the panel studying depression in later life from the NIH Consensus Development Conference.  Concise and to the point information about late life depression.

MH49   Neurobiology of Aging, Special Issue: Controversial topics on Alzheimer's disease: Intersecting Crossroads, V. 7, 1986.
       The issue discusses many of the present day theories as to the etiology of Alzheimer's Disease.

MH50   Newmann, J. P. (1989).  Aging and depression.  Psychology and Aging, 4, 150-165.
       Comprehensive review article examining the relationship of depression to the aging process.

MH51   Nolen-Hoeksema, S. (1988).  Life span views on depression.  In P. B. Baltes, D. L. Featherman & R. L. Lerner (Eds.), Life-span development and behavior: V. 9 (pp. 204-243).  Hillsdale, NJ: Lawrence Erlbaum.
       Discusses similarities and differences in the causes of depression across age, with attention to the role than life events across the life span play in causing major depressive episodes.

MH52   Oliver, O., & Bock, F. A. (1987).  Coping with Alzheimer's: A caregivers emotional survivor guide.  North Hollywood, FL: Wilshire Book Co.
       Well done personalized discussion of caregiver stress and coping, written from a cognitive behavioral perspective.

MH53   Parmelee, P. A., & Lawton, M. P. (1990).  The design of special environments for the aged.  Handbook of the psychology of aging (pp. 465-489).  New York: Academic Press.
       Explores the psychosocial significance of the environment in late life, emphasizing the contributions of aging research in optimizing person-environment fits.

MH54   Rodeheaver, D., & Datan, N. (1988).  The challenge of double jeopardy: Toward a mental health agenda for aging women.  American Psychologist, 43, 648-654.
       Examines the difficulties older women face in light of the many unique experiences and stresses they face and their implications for mental health care.

MH55    Roybal, E. R. (1988). Mental health and aging: The need for an expanded federal response. <u>American Psychologist</u>, <u>43</u>, 189-194.

       Examines the need for federal support for mental health services for older adults. Interestingly presented perspective from a non-psychologist.

MH56    Ruver, B. W., Katz, I. R. (1993). Psychiatric disorders in the nursing home: A selective review of studies. <u>International Journal of Geriatric Psychiatry</u>, <u>8</u>, 75-87.

       The authors review studies related to the clinical care of the elderly who live in nursing homes. Results indicate that most elderly in these types of setting have psychiatric disorders but that the training of staff and physicians and the recognition and the treatment of such disorders is very limited.

MH57    Seltzer, B., & Buswell, A. (1994). Psychiatric symptoms in Alzheimer's disease: Mental status examination versus caregiver report. <u>The Gerontologist</u>, <u>34</u>, 103-109.

       The purpose of this study was to examine the possible reasons for the differing prevalence rates of psychiatric feature reported in patients with Alzheimer's disease. Results indicated considerable differences in the report of psychiatric symptoms between formal mental status examination and a caregiver questionnaire. The physicians conducting the mental status exams reported less depression, lack of insight, apathy, anxiety, disinhibition, and overactivity.

MH58    Smyer, M. A., & Walls, C. T. (1994). Design and evaluation of interventions in nursing homes. In C. B. Fisher & R. M. Lerner (Eds.), <u>Applied developmental psychology</u> (pp. 475-501). New York: McGraw-Hill.

       This broadly focused chapter describes the nursing home industry and the roles it plays in the lives of older adults and their families. A specific intervention program designed to affect staff job performance and resident outcomes is described.

# 10

# *Personality*

P1    Abrams, R. C. (1991). The aging personality. <u>International Journal of Geriatric Psychiatry</u>, <u>6</u>, 1-3.
        The author argues that the pivotal problem in personality research on older adults is the selection of appropriate personality traits. The extent to which certain standardized ideas of personality can be applied to the elderly is discussed.

P2    Aiken, L. R. (1988). <u>Later life</u> (2nd ed.). Hillsdale, NJ: Lawrence Erlbaum Associates.
        This book focuses on the psychology of later life by identifying and reviewing the what is known in the field and by also describing the methods by which such information was obtained. The author includes a chapter entitled "Adjustment and personality."

P3    Alwin, D. F. (1994). Aging, personality, and social change: The stability of individual differences across the life span. In D. L. Featherman, R. M. Lerner & M. Perlmutter (Eds.), <u>Life-span development and behavior V. 12</u> (pp. 136-187). Hillsdale, NJ: Lawrence Erlbaum.
        Discusses the varying definitions of stability and their implications for the development of personality and intelligence over the life course.

P4    Atchley, R. C. (1982). The aging self. <u>Psychotherapy, Theory, Research, and Practice</u>, <u>19</u>, 388-396.
        The author reviews and organizes literature on aging and the self, while providing a framework by which future research might be more

effective. He discusses the a theory of how older adults maintain a positive self image when they are often times bombarded with negative evaluations.

P5     Baltes, P. B., Smith, J., Staudinger, U., & Sowarka, D. (1990). Wisdom : One facet of successful aging? In K. W. Schaie (Ed.), Annual review of gerontology and geriatrics: V. 7 (pp. 63-82). New York: Springer.

        Describes the research program at Max Planck Institute dealing with the measurement and understanding of the construct of wisdom. An interesting and engaging chapter.

P6     Berger, K. S. (1988). The developing person throughout the life span (2nd ed.). New York: Worth.

        The overall format of this text is chronological, dividing the life span into seven parts: infancy, early childhood, middle childhood, adolescence, early adulthood, middle adulthood, and late adulthood. The author has included a section in the text focused on personality throughout adulthood.

P7     Blanchard-Fields, F. (1994). Age differences in causal attributions from an adult developmental perspective. Journal of Gerontology: Psychological Sciences, 49, 43-51.

        This paper examines age differences in either person or situation attributions for performance in different types of situations varying by ambiguity and valence of outcome. Results suggests age effects in the quality of attributions persons make depend upon the nature of the situation, with older adults making more person and situation interaction attributions in situations involving relationships and in more negative outcome situations, making more attributions emphasizing qualities of the person.

P8     Brandstadter, J., & Renner, G. (1990). Tenacious goal pursuit and flexible goal adjustment, explication and age-related analysis of assimilative and accommodative strategies of coping. Psychology and Aging, 5, 58-67.

        Examines adjustment to life transitions in light of both passive and active styles of coping, finding that each predict life satisfaction. With age, there is a shift from an assimilative to an accommodative mode of coping.

P9     Brandstadter, J., & Rothermund, K. (1994). Self-percepts of control in middle and later adulthood: Buffering losses by rescaling goals. Psychology and Aging, 9, 265-273.

One of a series of papers by the first author illustrating how, with increasing age, adults preserve their self esteem and self efficacy by varying the importance and aspiration level of experiences and goals.

P10  Britton, P. G. (1989). Clinical psychology with the elderly: Aspects of intellectual functioning, personality, and adjustment. In K. Davidson & A. Kerr (Eds.), Contemporary themes in psychiatry: A tribute to Sir Martin Roth (pp. 291-298). London: Gaskell/Royal College of Psychiatrists.

This chapter presents work which has been done by clinical psychologists working under Sir Martin Roth. The knowledge presented deals with the processes of aging in terms of intellect and personality and how such information has been used to aid in the treatment of abnormalities of aging.

P11  Cantor, N., & Killstrom, J. F. (1987). Personality and social intelligence. Englewood Cliffs, NJ: Prentice-Hall.

This innovative text redefines social intelligence as a central part of personality enabling adults to deal with life tasks. The social context to which persons must adapt is given new emphasis in this novel approach to personality in adulthood.

P12  Caspi, A., & Bem, D. J. (1990). Personality continuity and change across the life course. In L. A. Pervin (Ed.), Handbook of personality: Theory and research (pp. 549-575). New York: Guilford.

Defines stability in several ways and discusses their implications for personality development across the life span.

P13  Caspi, A., & Elder, G. (1986). Life satisfaction in old age; linking social psychology and history. Psychology and Aging, 1, 18-26.

This valuable longitudinal study found that among the Berkeley sample, having good adaptive skills predicted life satisfaction 30 years later, depending on social class.

P14  Costa, P. T., Jr., & McCrae, R. R. (1991). Personality continuity and the changes in adult life. In P.T. Costa, M. Gatz, B.L. Neugarten, T.A. Salthouse, & I.C. Siegler (Eds.), The adult years: Continuity and change (pp. 45-77).

Presents an overview of personality and aging, emphasizing a trait perspective toward theory and measurement.

P15  Costa, P. T., Jr., Metter, E. J., & McCrae, R. R. (1994). Personality stability and its contribution to successful aging. Journal of Geriatric Psychiatry, 27, 41-60.

The authors provide a definition of personality based on enduring dispositions. They discuss the stability of these dispositions based on longitudinal studies which also indicate that this stability is an important contributor to psychological well-being. In addition, they show how the stability of personality contributes to successful aging.

P16     Cummings, E. M., Greene, A. L., & Karcaker, K. H. (1991). Life span developmental psychology: Perspectives on stress and coping. Hillsdale, NJ: Lawrence Erlbaum.

While this edited volume covers the entire life span, specific chapters devoted to theory, coping with negative life events, and personality and coping in late life are quite relevant. The last chapter discussing the entire collection is very valuable.

P17     Dalakishvili, S. M., Bakhtadze, I. A., & Nikuradze, M. D. A study of personality traits in old age. (1989). Soviet Journal of Psychology, 10, 80-89.

The authors investigated the personality set in old age by surveying elderly subjects as compared to younger subjects. In terms of apparent age related changes, older adults showed high emotional excitability, superficially explosive reactions, and lability of motives. Older adults also appeared to have high ability for adaptation to the environment.

P18     Elder, G. H. (1979). Historical change in life patterns and personality. In P. B. Baltes, O. Brim (Eds.), Life-span development and behavior: V 2 (pp. 117-139). New York: Academic Press.

Examines personality development in adulthood in the context of cohort effects, with attention to the impact of the 1930 depression. It contrasts with traditional approaches to personality and aging.

P19     Field, D., & Millsap, R. E. (1991). Personality in advanced old age: Continuity or change? Journal of Gerontology, 46, 299-308.

The authors conducted a longitudinal study of elderly persons and found evidence of personality development in advanced old age. Five traits, similar to traits found in younger persons, were identified. Although considerable continuity was found, change also appeared with an increase in agreeableness in old-old and a decrease in extraversion in both groups. Satisfaction and Intellect were found to be stable.

P20     Folkman, S. (1988). Coping across the lifespan: Theoretical issues. In E. M. Cummings, A. L. Greene & K. H. Karraker (Eds.), Life-span developmental psychology: Perspectives on stress and coping (pp. 3-20). Hillsdale, NJ: Lawrence Erlbaum.

Discusses several models of coping, and views the process of coping from within the contextual perspective. The process of coping is then discussed developmentally.

P21     Friedman, R. S. (1993). When the patient intrudes on the treatment: The aging of personality types in medical management. Journal of Geriatric Psychiatry, 26, 149-177.
        The author begins by addressing the relation of geriatric psychiatry and consultation-liaison psychiatry. He then describes how the personality changes with aging and how this process affects the patient's response to illness and treatment. In addition, he looks at how the treatments system responds to the older adults with medical illness.

P22     George, L. K. (1990). Social structure, social processes and socio-psychological states. In R. H. Binstock & L. K. George (Eds.), Handbook of aging and the social sciences (pp. 186-204). New York: Academic Press.
        This chapter explores the social psychology of later life in light of social/cultural structure, role theory, life events analysis, age stratification and modernization, using well being and the self as prototypes for discussion.

P23     Hayslip, Jr., B. (1988). Personality-ability relationships in aged adults. Journal of Gerontology, 43, 79-84.
        In an effort to investigate personality-ability interrelationships in older persons, 102 community-residing elderly persons were administered the Holtzman Inkblot Technique (HIT) and measures of both crystallized (Gc) and fluid (Gf) intelligence. Results suggested that each ability factor loaded on separate personality dimensions established in a previous analysis of HIT data using this sample.

P24     Henry, W. E., & Cumming, E. (1992). Personality development in adulthood and old age. In E. I. Megargee & C. D. Spielberger (Eds.), Personality assessment in America: A retrospective on the occasion of the fiftieth anniversary of the Society for Personality Assessment (pp. 79-86). Hillsdale, NJ: Lawrence Erlbaum Associates.
        The authors discuss how much of the written work about aging evaluates old age using an inappropriate middle-age frame of reference. They suggest, citing longitudinal studies using the TAT, that people's needs and values evolve over the life span with older adults tending to shift from an active to a more passive orientation.

P25     Kogan, N. (1990). Personality and aging. Handbook of the psychology of aging (pp. 330-346). New York: Academic Press.

Examines various theoretical models of personality and aging emphasizing the methodological aspects of research.

P26    Krueger, J., & Heckhausen, J. (1993). Personality development across the adult life span: Subjective conceptions vs. cross-sectional contrasts. Journals of Gerontology: Psychological Sciences, 48, 100-108.

Examines self vs. other oriented perceptions of personality change, wherein the positive and negative attributes of personality were rated across decades by adults in terms of a number of characteristics. While declines characterized later in life, characteristics attributed to personality were still positive in nature. In contrast, cross-sectional self-assessments suggested stability of personality.

P27    Lawton, M. P. (1983). Environment and other determinants of well-being in older people. The Gerontologist, 23, 349-357.

The dimensions of "the good life" are described, as are the relation-ships among them. Thorough discussion of measurement approaches to each dimension.

P28    Malatesta-Magai, C., Jonas, R., Shepard, B., & Culver, L. C. (1992). Type A behavior pattern and emotional expression in younger and older adults. Psychology and Aging, 7, 551-561.

Older and younger Type A and Type B individuals participated in the Structured Interview and were evaluated for Type A tendencies. The greatest differences were between ages with older subjects being more expressive than younger adults. In addition, women had more conflict in expressing anger and Type A women had more conflict in expressing anger than did Type A men.

P29    Manheimer, R. J. (1992). In search of the gerontological self. Journal of Aging Studies, 6, 319-332.

This article reviews the different theories of the gerontolgical self and was prompted by a conversation the author had with a frail, aging friend whose personality appeared very stable. The author discusses four approaches to the concept of self which include the humanist self, the behavioral self, the post-modernists' views of aging, and the phenomenological self.

P30    McAdams, D. P., St. Aubin, E., & Logan, R. L. (1993). Generativity among young, midlife, and older adults. Psychology and Aging, 8, 221-230.

Looking at various aspects of Erikson's construct of generativity, these authors found mixed support for the notion that generativity peaks at midlife. However, generativity and life satisfaction were positively related.

P31     McCrae, R. R. (1989).  Age differences and changes in the use of coping mechanisms. Journal of Gerontology: Psychological Sciences, 44, 161-169.
        Based on adults' identification of an event as a loss, threat, or challenge, both age and cohort effects were found in the use of coping mechanisms.  Yet longitudinal and sequential analyses suggested that age had little effect on the use of such skills.

P32     McCrae, R. R., & Costa, P. T. (1990).  Personality in adulthood. New York: Guilford Press.
        Overview of personality development in the adult years with a focus on the issue of stability vs. change from primarily a trait psychology perspective, though other points of view are discussed as well.

P33     McFarland, C., Ross, M., & Giltrow, M. (1992). Biased recollections in older adults: The role of implicit theories of aging. Journal of Personality and Social Psychology, 62, 837-850.
        This study used retrospective methodology in which subjects were asked to remember the personality traits they possessed at an earlier age.  The authors hypothesized that the older adults' recollections would be related to their theories and ideas of aging.  For traits that were thought to decrease with age, older adults reported having more when they were younger.  For traits that were thought to increase with age, older adults reported having lower levels at a younger age.

P34     Montepare, J. M., & Lachman, M. E. (1989). "You're only as old as you feel." Self-perceptions of age, fears of aging, and life satisfaction from adolescence to old age. Psychology and Aging, 4, 73-78.
        Examines "personal age" among adults aged 14-83, finding that relative to the young, those who were middle aged and older had younger subjective identities relative to their actual age.  For the young, fear of aging seemed to explain such discrepancies.

P35     Mortimer, J. T., Finch, M. D., & Kumka, D. (1982). Persistence and change in development: The multidimensional self-concept.  In P. B. Baltes & O. G. Brim, Jr. (Eds.), Life-span development and behavior: V. 4 (pp. 264-315).  New York: Academic Press.
        Discusses issues of stability and change in the development of self concept, taking a multidimensional approach.  This chapter argues for a reciprocal relationship between life events and the changing aspects of the self.

P36     Mueller, J. H., Johnson, W. C., Dandoy, A., & Keller, T. (1992). Trait distinctiveness and age specificity in the self-concept. In R. P.

Lipka & T. M. Brinthaupt (Eds.), Self-perspectives across the life span (pp. 223-255). Albany, NY: New York Press.

The authors of this chapter examine the differences in self-concept and self awareness between young and old adults. Relationships between self-concept and memory and age-specific traits are also discussed.

P37     Neugarten, B. L. (1977). Personality and aging. In J. E. Birren & K. W. Schaie (Eds.), Handbook of the psychology of aging (pp. 626-649). New York: Van Nostrand Reinhold.

Noteworthy chapter detailing evidence bearing on pivotal questions regarding the mutual relationships between personality and aging.

P38     Thomaé, H. (1992). Emotion and personality. In J. E. Birren, R. B. Sloane, & G. D. Cohen (Eds.), Handbook of mental health and aging (2nd ed.) (pp. 355-375). San Diego: Academic Press.

Discusses change and stability with age in various emotional behavioral and emotional dispositions as well as interrelationships among personality and intelligence in later life.

P39     Whitbourne, S. K. (1987). Personality development in adulthood and old age: Relationships between identity style, health, and well-being. In K. W. Schaie (Ed.), Annual Review of Gerontology and Geriatrics: V. 7) (pp. 189-216). New York: Springer.

Focuses on the identity styles of accomodative assimilative and balanced on their implications for adjustment to the aging process.

P40     Wrightsman, L. S. (1988). Personality development in adulthood. Newbury Park, CA: Sage.

Well written but basic presentation of the major theoretical approaches to personality as well as chapters dealing with sex roles, marriage and sexuality, values and attitude change, and death.

P41     Wrightsman, L. S. (1994). Adult personality development: Theories and concepts. Newbury Park: CA: Sage Publications.

First of 2 volumes examining a variety of theoretical approahces to personality development ranging from Erikson to Riegel.

P42     Wrightsman, L. S. (1994). Adult personality development: Applications. Newbury Park, CA: Sage Publications.

Explores specific domains of personality e.g., occupational, cognitive, sex role-related, values and attitudes, as they vary across the life span.

# 11

# *Therapy and Intervention*

TH1     Atkinson, D. R., & Hackett, G. (Eds.). (1988). Counseling non-ethnic American minorities. Springfield, IL: Charles C. Thomas, Publisher.
        This book discusses the therapeutic needs and possible strategies for working with the disabled, elderly, women and gay people. In addition to providing the rationale for identifying the groups as minorities and a profile of each group, the authors discusses the past failures of traditional psychotherapy with these groups.

TH2     Bowlby, M. C. (1993). Therapeutic activities with persons disabled by Alzheimer's disease and related disorders. Gaithersburg, MD: Aspen.
        This book provides a variety of treatments for persons with Alzheimer's disease and related disorders. These treatments are designed to enable individuals with AD to accomplish their final life tasks, to affirm their personhood, and to reaffirm the value of their previous life experiences.

TH3     Bradbury, N. (1991). Problems of elderly people. In W. Dryden & R. R. Rentoul (Eds.), Adult clinical problems: A cognitive-behavioral approach (pp. 203-231). London: Routledge.
        This chapter addresses the issues that older adults are subject to all the psychological problems experienced by adults of any age, but does explain problems which are more likely to be faced in later life such as depression, dealing with chronic illness, and abnormal grief. Emphasis is given to the special considerations when using cognitive behavioral techniques with older adults.

TH4     Brammer, L. M. (1984). Counseling theory and the older adult. The
        Counseling Psychologist, 12, 29-37.
             The author addresses the idea that counseling psychologists lack
        experience with older adults and emphasizes the importance of adapting
        and broadening traditional theories and contemporary mini-theories to
        encompass the growing population of older adults. This paper begins
        this process of expansion by exploring the contributions and limitations
        of various families of theories using specific names of major contribu-
        tors. Theories and theorists were selected to be representative rather
        than exhaustive.

TH5     Brody, C. M., & Semel, V. G. (1993). Strategies for therapy with the
        elderly: Living with hope and meaning. New York: Springer.
             The overall message of this book is that older adults can benefit
        from therapy whether they are living in a nursing home, in semi-
        independent housing, or living independently. The book describes
        therapy for elderly women and men and encompasses a variety of
        approaches, ranging from eclectic approaches to be used in nursing
        homes to psychoanalytic techniques to be used with elderly clients in
        individual therapy.

TH6     Burnside, I. (Ed.), & Schimidt, M. G. (Ed.). (1994). Working with
        older adults: Group process and techniques (3rd ed.). Boston: Jones
        and Barlett.
             This third edition is different from the first two in that a new co-
        editor with a social work perspective has been added. The book does
        not simple address group dynamics, but describes the types of groups
        which can be used in a variety of settings. Topics discussed include the
        history of group work, theoretical frameworks, organizational
        guidelines, clinical modalities, settings for group work, multidisciplin-
        ary perspectives, and clinical and educational issues.

TH7     Casey, D. A., & Grant, R. W. (1993). Cognitive therapy with
        depressed elderly patients. In J. H. Wright, M. E. Thase, A. T. Beck,
        & J. W. Ludgate (Eds.), Cognitive therapy with inpatients: Developing
        a cognitive milieu (pp. 295-314). New York: Guilford.
             This chapter discusses the use of cognitive therapy with elderly
        depressives and introduces the concept of supportive cognitive therapy.
        The authors offer an informal means of presenting CT in the inpatient
        setting which would reach individuals who would not otherwise be seen
        as candidates for therapy.

TH8     Flint, A. J. (1992). The optimum duration of antidepressant treatment
        in the elderly. International Journal of Geriatric Psychiatry, 7, 617-619.

The author discusses data on the optimum duration of antidepressant treatment in elderly patients and suggests that the standard 6 months of treatment may be too brief for the elderly population.

TH9    Genevay, B., & Katz, R. S. (1990). Countertransference and older clients. Newbury Park, CA: Sage.
       Unique volume written from the therapists' view in dealing with feelings and reactions to working with older adults. Specific chapters deal with the dying process, AIDS, suicide, disability, dementia, substance abuse, and caregiving.

TH10   Goodstein, R. K. (1982). Individual psychotherapy and the elderly. Psychotherapy: Theory, Research, and Practice, 19, 412-418.
       The author addresses the issue that older adults bring to therapy a greater number of life experiences and interests which provide the basis for strong transference and countertransference. He highlights the need for counselors to prepare for the fears and needs that are common for older individuals. Discussion also includes suggested adjustments in therapy to be considered when seeing older clients.

TH11   Haight, B. K. (1992). Long-term effects of a structured life review process. Journals of Gerontology, 47, 312-315.
       The author examined the long-terms effects of a structured life review process in a group of homebound older adults. Those subjects involved in the life review increased in their life satisfaction and psychological well-being after 8 weeks. Information gathered at a 1 year follow-up is also discussed.

TH12   Hayslip, B., & Caraway, M. (1989). Cognitive therapy with aged persons: Implications of research design for its implementation and evaluation. Journal of Cognitive Psychotherapy: An International Quarterly, 3, 255-271.
       Critically evaluates research on cognitive therapy and aging in light of several principles of experimental and developmental research methods.

TH13   Hayslip, B., Schneider, L., & Bryant, K. (1989). Older women's perceptions of female counselors: The influence of therapist age and problem intimacy. The Gerontologist, 29, 239-244.
       This study explored perceptions of younger and older counselors in older women, finding some evidence for an age effect, but a stronger effect for age preferences as a function of the intimacy value of what was discussed in therapy.

TH14    Kim, P. K. H. (Ed.). (1991). <u>Serving the elderly: Skills for practice.</u>
        New York: Aldine de Gruyter.
              This book offers information on seven important approaches to
        working with older adults including counseling, family therapy,
        reminiscent therapy, validation therapy, behavioral therapy, rational
        self-help counseling, and the small group approach. Discussion is also
        included concerning social planning, management and administration,
        program evaluation, consultation, and fund raising.

TH15    Knight, B. (1986). <u>Psychotherapy with older adults</u>. Newbury Park,
        CA: Sage.
              This book discusses many of the critical issues involved in psycho-
        therapy with older adults. Topics included are adaptations in therapy,
        making contact with the client, general assessment issues, major
        therapy themes and topics, transference and countertransference,
        families of the elderly and systems-level interventions. The author
        writes in a very readable manner, incorporating case examples.

TH16    Knight, B. (1992). <u>Older adults in psychotherapy: Case histories</u>.
        Newbury Park, CA: Sage.
              This book contains a number of case histories of elderly clients in
        therapy. After each description, the author offers a discussion section
        including issues of rapport building, techniques in therapy, gerontologi-
        cal issues, relationship issues. He then ends each case with a brief
        summary. The author speaks in a very candid and helpful manner
        about his reactions as a therapist.

TH17    Langley, D. (1987). Dramatherapy with elderly people. In S. Jennings
        (Ed.), <u>Dramatherapy: Therapy and practice for teachers and clinicians</u>
        (pp. 233-256). London: Croom Helm.
              This chapter focuses on the application of dramatherapy with aging
        people. The author focuses on Reality Orientation and Reminiscence
        Theatre.

TH18    Lauber, B. M., & Drevenstedt, J. (1993). Older adults' preference for
        age and sex of a therapist. <u>Clinical Gerontologist</u>, <u>12</u>, 13-26.
              Through the use of video-taped counseling vignettes, the authors
        obtained older adults preferences for therapists varying in age and sex.
        Results indicated that older adults preferred older counselors with
        females preferring females and males in indicating no preference.
        Some of the implications for older adults' use of mental health services
        are discussed.

TH19    Lawton, M. P. (1990). Residential environment and self-directedness among older people. American Psychologist, 45, 638-640.
        Discusses the design of nursing homes and housing in general with special attention to ways for which the frailties of aging might be compensated.

TH20    Lazarus, L. W., & Sadavoy, J. (1988). Psychotherapy with the elderly. In L. W. Lazarus (Ed.), Essentials of geriatric psychiatry: A guide for health professionals (pp. 147-172). New York: Springer.
        This chapter discusses some of the developmental challenges of late life and describes some of the barriers to getting elderly people involved in therapy. Discussion also centers on the common problems older adults will present with and various psychotherapeutic techniques which might be employed such as individual, family, or group therapy. The chapter ends with the results from some recent outcome studies.

TH21    MacLennan, B. W., Saul, S., & Weiner, M. B. (Eds.). (1988). Group psychotherapies for the elderly. Madison, CT: International Universities Press.
        This volume begins with a review of group therapy with older adults. The following sections focus on insight group therapy, supportive/rehabilitative group therapy in the community, and supportive group therapy in institutions. The use of art in therapy and a possible training technique are also discussed.

TH22    McKitrick, D. (1981). Counseling dying clients. Omega, 12, 165-187.
        This paper reviews approaches to individual counseling with adult dying clients. The potential strengths and weaknesses of each approached are discussed. The author highlights the importance of matching the approach with the individual client. Clients are categorized in terms of Kastenbaum and Aisenberg's four ways of responding to one's death: overcoming, participating, fearing, and sorrowing.

TH23    Morris, R. G., & Morris, L. W. (1991). Cognitive and behavioral approaches with the depressed elderly. Special Issue: Affective disorders in old age. International Journal of Geriatric Psychiatry, 6, 407-413.
        The authors present an approach to working with depressed older clients. This approach involves maintaining a flexible approach and accounting for the experiential background of the elderly. Therapies they promote are behavioral therapy, cognitive therapy, problem solving, skills training, and reminiscence.

TH24   Muslin, H. L. (1992). The psychotherapy of the elderly self. New
       York: Brunner/Mazel.
           This book dispels aging myths and focuses on old age as a natural
       developmental phase. In addition, the author offers an effective model
       of observation, diagnosis, and therapy for working with older adults.
       According to the forward of the book, the author's task is to demon-
       strate that therapy, including psychoanalysis, has an important role in
       relieving suffering and promoting growth in the elderly.

TH25   Myers, W. A. (Ed.). (1991). New techniques in the psychotherapy of
       older patients. Washington, D. C.: American Psychiatric Press.
           This book offers a clinical as well as theoretical review of a great
       variety of psychotherapeutic techniques used with older patients. The
       first section of the book focuses on time-limited therapies, the second
       on short-term and longer term techniques, and the third and last portion
       describes the longer-term treatments such as group therapy and psycho-
       analysis.

TH26   Newton, N. A., Brauer, D., Gutmann, D. L., & Grunes, J. (1986).
       Psychodynamic therapy with the aged: A review. Clinical Gerontolo-
       gist, 5, 205-229.
           The authors begin with a theoretical review of psychodynamic
       perspectives potentially related to aging (e.g., neo Freudian, develop-
       mental, self-psychology). They describe the potential impact of aging
       in terms of an increased focus on the Self, a redistribution of libido,
       and regression. According to the authors, psychodynamic therapy with
       older adults centers on developing insight, especially awareness of
       intrapsychic processes. The therapist must project more empathy, be
       more active, less formal and be more flexible in scheduling and
       terminating than is traditionally allowed in psychoanalysis.

TH27   Parham, I. A., Priddy, J. M., McGovern, T. V., & Richman, C. M.
       (1982). Group psychotherapy with the elderly: Problems and pros-
       pects. Psychotherapy: Theory, Research, and Practice, 19, 437-443.
           The authors review the development of group psychotherapy with
       the elderly over a 30-year period beginning in 1950. They discuss the
       strengths and weaknesses of the research generated during this period.
       Discussion centers on the critical elements of group psychotherapy with
       older adults and what makes it effective.

TH28   Richardson, V. E. (1993). Retirement Counseling: A handbook for
       gerontology practitioners. New York: Springer.
           In this book the author provides practitioners with techniques to be
       used with retirees who are having difficulty adjusting. Discussion

includes information concerning the conceptual issues in retirement, the generic model for retirement intervention, and the heterogeneity of the retirement experience.

TH29    Sadavoy, J., Lazarus, L. W., & Jarvik, L. F. (eDS.). (1991). Comprehensive review of geriatric psychiatry. Washington, D. C.: American Psychiatric Press.
        This comprehensive volume contains chapters on group therapy, family therapy, individual psychotherapy, and electroconvulsive therapy with older adults.

TH30    Sadavoy, J., & Leszcz, M. (Eds.). (1987). Treating the elderly with psychotherapy: The scope for change in later life. Madison, CT: International Univ.
        This book focuses on many disorders and geriatric patients in a variety of settings. The emphasis is on presenting psychodynamic and psychotherapeutic theories and techniques as practical with older persons on a clinical level. The book could prove useful to anyone who may be involved in an interdisciplinary team.

TH31    Sadavoy, J., & Robinson, A. (1989). Psychotherapy and the cognitively impaired elderly. In D. K. Conn, A. Grek, & J. Sadavoy (Eds.), Psychiatric consequences of brain disease in the elderly: A focus on management (pp. 101-135). New York: Plenum.
        The authors of this chapter review some of the frequently used therapeutic approaches to the demented elderly, but restrict their review to those approaches which utilize interaction and communication. After this review, the authors use a case study to explore the question--what remains of the personality and the self as the mind dements?

TH32    Silva, J. A., & Leiderman, P. H. The life-span approach to individual therapy: An overview with case presentation. In P. Baltes, D. Featherman, & R. Lerner (Eds.), Life-span development and behavior: V. 7 (pp. 114-135). Hillsdale, NJ: Lawrence Erlbaum.
        The authors present a case example of the application of the life-span perspective to the therapy and treatment of a 63-year-old man who experienced the Bataan Death March in the Philippines and 3 1/2 years in Japanese prison camps during WWII. The therapeutic techniques ranged from psychodynamic to the use of more objective information such as ethnographic and historical materials from the patient's childhood community.

TH33   Simmons, H. C., & Pierce, V. S. (1992). <u>Pastoral responses to older</u>
<u>adults and their families: An annotated bibliography</u>. Westport, CT:
Greenwood Press.
   Comprehensive resource detailing published resources focusing on
a variety of topics dealing with the pastoral care of older adults. It
includes specific chapters on ethics, life review, and death and dying.

TH34   Smyer, M. A., Zarit, S. H., & Qualls, S. H. (1990). Psychological
intervention with the aging individual. <u>Handbook of the psychology of</u>
<u>aging</u> (pp. 375-404). New York: Academic Press.
   Excellent overview of issues underlying the variety of psychological
treatments for elderly adults, with attention to the efficacy of such
interventions. Public policy and funding issues are also addressed.

TH35   Steenbarger, B. N. (1991). All the world is not a stage: Emerging
contextualist themes in counseling and development. <u>Journal of</u>
<u>Counseling & Development</u>, <u>70</u>, 288-296.
   The author discusses the shortcomings of classical stage-based
theories of human development when extended to counseling applications. He suggests that counselors are turning to contextual models of
development that emphasize process over outcome. The article
contains a review of the key assumptions of contextualism, as embodied
in social role theory and the life-span developmental tradition,
highlighting relevant theory and research. Discussion ends with
specific implications of contextualism for future counseling research
and practice.

TH36   Stone, J. D. (1987). Marital and sexual counseling of elderly couples.
In G. R. Weeks & L. Hof (Eds.), <u>Integrating sex and marital therapy:</u>
<u>A clinical guide</u> (pp. 221-244). New York: Brunner/Mazel.
   This chapter offers a discussion of therapy with elderly couples. It
touches on the aging process, assessment, and goal planning and
provides possible treatment considerations.

TH37   Tuseland, R. W. (1990). <u>Group work with older adults</u>. New York:
New York University Press.
   The book offers information on group work with well and frail
elderly in community and institutional settings. Topics addressed
include the history of group work, group dynamics, leadership skills,
and specific skills, procedures, and techniques to be used with
specialized groups such as support groups and educational groups.
Each chapter of the book contain a case example illustrating the
information in the chapter.

TH38    Viney, L. L. (1993). Life stories: Personal construct therapy with the
        elderly. Chichester, England: John Wiley & Sons.
           The author discusses the importance older adults attribute to the
        telling of their life stories and explains how the reaction of others to
        these stories can have tremendous effects on the well-being of older
        adults.  She provides an approach to therapy which encompasses the
        importance of such stories, case studies of how this therapy has
        worked, and strategies to keep in mind when using it.

TH39    Waters, E. B. (1984). Building on what you know: Techniques for
        individual and group counseling with older people. The Counseling
        Psychologist, 12, 63-74.
           This article delineates some of the similarities and differences in
        working with older and younger people in counseling. It also identifies
        some of the major modalities followed in working with the elderly.
        While many basic skills are the same, adaptations must be made to take
        into account the broader life experiences which older people have had
        and the increased likelihood of sensory and other losses. It highlights
        the value of group work in helping older adults improve their social
        skills, reduce loneliness, and discover commonalities with their peers.

TH40    Weiner, M. B., Brok, A. J., & Snadowsky, A. M. (1987). Working
        with the aged: Practical approaches in the institution and the communi-
        ty. Norwalk, CT: Appleton-Century Crofts.
           Narrowly focused volume dealing with intervention and psychothera-
        peutic techniques for use with institutionalized and community aged
        persons.

TH41    Wisocki, P. A. (Ed.). (1991). Handbook of clinical behavior therapy
        with the elderly client: Applied clinical psychology. New York:
        Plenum.
           This text has sections on the behavioral approach to aging, factors
        affecting treatment of the elderly, treatment applications, and interven-
        tions in the health and community care systems. The contributors are
        well known in the field. Some of the specific applications discussed
        include social training skills, stress management, assessment and treat-
        ment of depression, and pain management.

TH42    Wulinsky, M. A. (1986). Marital therapy with older couples. Social
        Casework, 67, 475-483.
           Discusses marital therapy for couples in long-standing marriages.
        A developmental marital model for mature-stage marriages is present-
        ed. Specific developmental tasks in the mature marriage are based on
        the time of life and lifestyle.

# 12

# *Assessment*

A1    Addington, J., & Fry, P.S. (1986). Directions for clinical-psychosocial assessment of depression in the elderly. <u>Clinical Gerontologist</u>, <u>5</u>, 97-117.

    The authors give a review of the many concerns involved in the assessment of geriatric depression, and stress the necessity for multidimensional assessment. The key issues they address are accurate assessment as the key to appropriate and effective intervention with the aged, the tests and symptoms used to identify depression in younger populations do not work with older individuals, and that the interaction of depression with physical ailments, and the problem of differential diagnosis with organic brain syndrome. The three perspectives to view depression in later life presented by the authors are the medical model, psychodynamic model and cognitive-behavioral model.

A2    Arnold, S. B. (1991). Measurement of quality of life in the frail elderly. In J. E. Birren, J. E. Lubben, J. C. Rowe, & D. E. Deutchman (Eds.), <u>The concept and measurement of quality of life in the frail elderly</u> (pp. 50-73). San Diego: Academic.

    This chapter is a review of the literature on quality of life measures with a focus on the appropriateness of using such measures with the frail elderly. The definition of quality of life and several current measures of quality of life are critically discussed in reference to frail elderly.

A3    Bellak, L., & Abrams, D. M. (1993). <u>The Thematic Apperception Test, the Children's Apperception Test, and the Senior Apperception Technique in clinical use</u> (5th ed.). Boston: Allyn & Bacon.

In addition to providing information on the TAT and CAT, the authors discuss relevant issues related to the use of the SAT. They suggest that it may be useful in assessing problems in older adults that can be addressed by physicians, social workers, and nurses not specifically trained in clinical psychology.

A4    Birren, J. E., Sloane, R. B., & Cohen, G. D. (Eds.). (1992). Handbook of mental health and aging. San Diego, CA: Academic.

As the premiere reference in the field of gerontology, this volume contains excellent information on assessment, treatment, and prevention. With respect to assessment, the specific chapters included focus on neuropsychiatric assessment, neuropsychological assessment, functional assessment, behavioral and psychotherapeutic interventions, psychopharmacologic treatment, and interventions for cognitively impaired older persons.

A5    Carroll, R. E., Curran, S. M., Ross, M., Murray, C., Riddle, W., Moffoot, A. P. R., Ebemeier, K. P., & Goodwin, G. M. (1994). The differentiation of major depression from dementia of the Alzheimer type using within-subject neuropsychological discrepancy analysis. British Journal of Clinical Psychology, 33, 23-32.

This study compared a variety of within-subject discrepancy analyses comparing premorbid estimates with current measures of memory and intellectual functioning across three groups: patients with Alzheimer's disease, patients with depression, and healthy controls. Although group differences were found, the researchers concluded that none of the simple neuropsychological discrepancy analyses could used in clinical practice to make differential diagnoses.

A6    Decalmer, P., Marriott, A., Ainsworth, D., Bamlett, R., & Cowley, J. (1993). The multidisciplinary assessment of clients and patients. In P. Decalmer & F. Glendenning (Eds.), The mistreatment of elderly people (pp. 117-135). London: Sage.

This chapter describes and gives some insight into how a multidisciplinary team approaches the assessment and treatment of cases of elder abuse. Case examples are included. The authors also offer ways in which each professional could use their expertise in forming strategies for care and intervention.

A7    Fillenbaum, G. G. (1988). Multidimensional functional assessment of older adults: The Duke Older Adults Americans Resources and Services procedure. Hillsdale, NJ: Lawrence Erlbaum.

This book traces the development of the Multidimensional Functional Assessment Questionnaire (MFAQ). It discusses the practical uses of the procedure for clinicians, program evaluators, and planners. The author offers information concerning psychometric structure, comparison norms, reliability and validity.

A8      Gallagher, D. (1986). The Beck Depression Inventory and older adults: Review of its development and utility. Clinical Gerontologist, 5, 149-163.

The author reviews the prevelance of use, validity, reliability, factor structure, and utility for screening, research, and symptom monitoring of the Beck Depression Inventory with the elderly.

A9      Gatz, M., Smyer, M. A., Garfein, A. J., & Seward, M. (1991). Essentials of assessment in long-term care settings. In M. S. Harper (Ed.), Management and care of the elderly: Psychosocial perspectives (pp. 293-309). Newbury Park, CA: Sage.

This chapter offers an introduction to the uses of assessment in nursing homes or other long-term care settings such as home health care agencies. The authors describe a set of assessment instruments that are currently being used and viewed as helpful. Discussion on the present assumptions about the assessment process is also included.

A10     Goss, C., & Harper, M. S. (1991). Assessing the elderly in the community for referral to health services. In M. S. Harper (Ed.), Management and care of the elderly: Psychosocial perspectives (pp. 332-339). Newbury Park, CA: Sage.

The authors of this chapter discuss the necessity of social service agencies to assess and respond to the changing needs of the elderly community. They offer a geriatric community nurse program as an example of an in-home assessment and referral service.

A11     Grohen, M. E. (1989). Modifications in assessment and treatment of the communicatively impaired elderly. In R. H. Hull & K. M. Griffin (Eds.), Communication disorders in aging (pp. 103-118). Newbury Park, CA: Sage.

The first section of this chapter offers a discussion of the variables in the behavior of elderly persons that affect test selection and administration. The second half contains suggestions for changing treatment plans if problems are found. Specific topics include assessment goals, testing environment, test selection, test administration, vision, fatigue, etc.

A12     Harkins, S. W., & Price, D. D. (1992). Assessment of pain in the elderly. In D. C. Turk & R. Melzack (Eds.), Handbook of pain assessment (pp. 315-331). New York: Guilford.

This chapter discusses the assessment of pain in the elderly. Discussion includes reasons to expect age changes in pain perception, methodological issues, and demography. Other topics include pain in the laboratory, pain prevalence in the elderly, chronic pain and age, chronic pain and depression, and treatment of geriatric pain.

A13     Hayslip, Jr., B., & Lowman, R. L. (1986). The clinical use of projective techniques with the aged: A critical review and synthesis. Clinical Gerontologist, 5, 63-93.

This paper offers an excellent comprehensive review of what has been done in the often neglected field of projective techniques in geriatric psychology. The authors discuss the value of projective techniques in assessing competency, need for institutionalization, suicidal risk, aggression, readiness for psychotherapy, etc. Stress is placed on the practitioner's talent and how the validity, reliability, and utility of the tests discussed pivots on the training and skill of the clinician. Tests discussed include the Rorschach, Thematic Apperception Test (and two versions designed for elders, the SAT and GAT), Holtzman Inkblot Technique, Figure Drawing, Hand Test, and Sentence Completion.

A14     Holden, U. (1988). Realistic assessment. In U. Holden (Ed.), Neuropsychology and aging: Definitions, explanations and practical approaches (pp. 23-50). New York: New York University.

This chapter focuses on simple assessment and lists some of the most obvious signs to be identified. The author provides a screening procedure and clearly emphasized the necessity of watching and listening throughout the assessment process. Topics discussed include preparation for the assessment, neuropsychological investigations and batteries, listening, watching, orientation, etc.

A15     Horton, A. M., Jr. (Ed.). (1990). Neuropsychology across the life span: Assessment and treatment. New York: Springer.

This book offers information on age-appropriate problems, assessment procedures, and interventions for patients across the life span. It provides a review of neuropsychological disorders, an overview of screening techniques for brain damage, and a review of behavioral and cognitive retraining intervention. The author states that he hopes the book will be helpful for a variety of professionals including geriatric psychiatrists and those in geropsychology training programs.

A16     Hunt, T., (Ed.) & Lindley, C.J. (Ed.). (1989). Testing older adults: A reference guide for geropsychological assessments. Austin, TX: PRO-ED.

This book is the fourth in a series focused on presenting a life-span approach to psychological tests. The book offers an understanding of the older person and the special considerations which need to be considered in the selection, administration, and interpreting of psychological tests with this population. In addition the authors provide information on the current state of the geropsychological testing field and offer what they consider to be the emerging critical issues in the field. One such issue they discuss is the evaluation of competency.

A17     Kazniak, A.W. (1990). Psychological assessment of the aging individual. Handbook of the psychology of aging (pp. 427-445). New York: Academic Press.

Research-oriented review of psychogerontological assessment. Neuropsychological and functional assessmsent as well as the assessment of memory complaints are given special attention, as are psychometrics.

A18     Kivela, S. L. (1992). Psychological assessment and rating scales: Depression and other age-related affective disorders. In M. Bergener, K. Hasegawa, S. I. Finkel, & T. Nishimura (Eds.), Aging and mental disorders (pp. 102-123). New York: Springer.

The author discusses the need for rating scales which are specifically designed for, or at least standardized in, older populations. In addition, some of the important issues to be considered when judging a scale usable with older adults are included. The author lists scales and interviews which seem appropriate for geriatric use.

A19     Koeppl, P. M., Bolla-Wilson, D., & Bleecker, M. L. (1989). The MMPI: Regional differences or normal aging. Journals of Gerontology, 44, 95-99.

The authors investigated the MMPI profiles of a number of health men and women in an attempt to determine whether or not separate norm tables are needed for older individuals. Results did not indicate the age related changes which previous research has reported.

A20     La Rue, A. (1986). Neuropsychological assessment of older adults. Clinical Psychologist, 39, 96-98.

The author discusses the appropriateness and possible need for neuropsychological evaluation to determine the nature and severity of many cognitive and emotional problems in older adults.

A21     Lacro, J. P., Harris, M. J., & Jeste, D. V. (1993). Late life psychosis. International Journal of Geriatric Psychiatry, 8, 49-57.

The authors of this article present a brief review of the results of recent research in late life psychosis (LLP). Their discussion includes the topics of late onset schizophrenia, older patients with early onset schizophrenia, delusional disorder, psychosis in patients with dementia, psychosis in patients with depression, and miscellaneous psychoses.

A22    Levy, R., Howard, R., & Burns, A. (Eds.). (1993). Treatment and care in old age psychiatry. Petersfield, England: Wrightson Biomedical Publishing.

This book is meant to be a guide for researchers and clinicians to the assessment, treatment and long-term care of elderly psychiatric patients. Topics discussed include depression, memory, sleep disorders, and dementia.

A23    Liang, J., & Whitelaw, N. A. (1990). Assessing the physical and mental health of the elderly. In S. M. Stahl (Ed.), The legacy of longevity: Health and health care in later life (pp. 35-54). Newbury Park, CA: Sage.

A number of critical issues involved in the assessment of physical and mental health. The authors discuss the conceptualization and measurement of health with special attention to the reliability and validity with reference to physical and mental health assessment in the elderly. In addition, the authors present their own efforts to integrate elements of physical and mental health of older adults.

A24    McCrae, R. R. (1991). The five-factor model and its assessment in clinical settings. Journal of Personality Assessment, 57, 399-414.

This article introduces the five factor model of personality traits (Neuroticism, Extraversion, Openness to Experience, Agreeableness, and Conscientiousness) and presents the NEO Personality Inventory (NEO-PI), a questionnaire designed to measure the factors and some of the traits that define them. Reliability, validity, and stability of measures of the factors are reviewed, and correlations between scales from the NEO-PI and the MMPI and MCMII are presented.

A25    McGadney, B. F., Goldberg-Glen, R., & Pinkston, E. M. (1987). Clinical issues for assessment and intervention with the Black elderly. In L. L. Carstensen & B. A. Edelstein (Eds.), Handbook of clinical gerontology (pp. 354-375). Elmsford, NY: Pergamon.

This chapter offers information for those clinicians who will likely provide mental health services to the black elderly. Topics discussed include ageism, racist biases, family structure, life cycle issues and intervention methods. The authors also discuss health services and mental health care issues related to the black elderly population.

A26     Olin, J. T., Schineider, L. S., Eaton, E. M., Zemansky, M. F., et al.
        (1992). The Geriatric Depression Scale and the Beck Depression
        Inventory as screening instruments in an older adult outpatient
        population. Psychological Assessment, 4, 190-192.
            The authors compared older adult outpatients with major depression
        and healthy controls using the Geriatric Depression Scale (GDS) and
        the Beck Depression Inventory (BDI). Although both scales appeared
        efficient in detecting clinical depression in older adults, results indicated
        that the GDS is likely simpler for older adults to complete.

A27     Oswald, W. D., & Fleischmann, U. M. (1984). Psychometrics in
        aging and dementia: Advances in geropsychological assessments.
        International Workshop: Psychiatry in aging and dementia. Archives
        of Gerontology, 4, 299-309.
            The authors describe the Nuremberg Gerontopsychological Inventory
        (NAI). The NAI is a set of psychological tests that includes standard-
        ized performance tests, observer ratings, self-ratings, and a personality
        rating. The authors suggest that such an inventory could reliably and
        validly evaluate changes in old age.

A28     Poon, L. W., Crook, T., Davis, K. L., Eisendorfer, C., Garland, B.
        J., Kaszniak, A. W. (Eds.), & Thompson, L. W. (Ed.). (1986).
        Handbook for clinical memory assessment of older adults. Washington,
        DC: American Psychological Association.
            This handbook discusses the underlying theoretical and clinical
        issues important in the selection of an assessment instrument or battery
        and the types of tests available. It is designed to provide direction for
        professionals to make informed decisions about memory assessment.
        The authors suggest that the information provided may be used when
        considering memory assessment in general.

A29     Priest, W. A., & Meunier, G. F. (1993). MMPI-2 performance of
        elderly women. Clinical Gerontologist, 14, 3-11.
            The authors found that the healthy well-educated women in their
        study showed the expected increase in L and decrease in 4, but did not
        show decreased energy levels or increased somatic concerns. They
        suggest that demographic variables may have an influence on MMPI
        profiles of older adults.

A30     Rubenstein, L. Z., & Wieland, D. (1990). Comprehensive geriatric
        assessment. In M. P. Lawton (Ed.), Annual review of gerontology and
        geriatrics, Vol. 9 (pp. 145-192). New York: Springer.
            This chapter critically reviews the literature on geriatric assessment
        and evaluates the evidence of its benefit. The authors identify problems

regarding geriatric assessment effectiveness and the geriatric assessment knowledge base. In addition, they offer directions for further research in the area.

A31    Rueben, D. B., & Siu, A. L. (1992). New approaches to functional assessment. In B. Vellas, J. L. Albarede, A. J. Campbell, J. G. Evans, D. Guez, F. J. Herrero, L. Rubenstein, L. G. Serro-Azul, H. Werner, et al. (Eds.), Facts and research in gerontology: 1992 (pp. 191-202). New York: Springer.

       This chapter reviews the recent advances in the development and validation of scales to measure physical function in community-dwelling elderly persons and presents ideas for their clinical and research use. The measures discussed range from those containing a few questions to those requiring props and personal administration.

A32    Thompson, L. W., Gong, V., Haskins, E., & Gallagher, D. (1987). Assessment of depression and dementia during the later years. In K. W. Schaie (Ed.), Annual review of gerontology and geriatrics (pp. 295-324). New York: Springer.

       This chapters focuses on the difficulty in distinguishing between depression and dementia. The authors review a number of instruments, rating scales, and structured interviews which could be useful in the assessment of this distinction. The authors also discuss the six areas of cognitive function which should be evaluated when making such a diagnostic decision.

A33    Ward, T., Dawe, B., Procter, A., Murphy, E., & Weinman, J. (1993). Assessment in severe dementia: The Guy's Advanced Dementia Schedule. Age and Ageing, 22, 183-189.

       This study describes the development of a schedule which is designed to distinguish between subjects based on their responses to a number of objects varying in familiarity. The subjects were asked to respond by either picking up, naming, or using the object. The measure discussed was found to be reliable and valid in relation to the Clifton Assessment Procedures for the Elderly and the Mini-Mental State Examination.

A34    Weiner, M. F. (Ed.). (1991). The dementias: Diagnosis and management. Washington, DC: American Psychiatric Press.

       This volume offers valuable information about all aspects of the diagnosis and management of dementia. While closely following the DSM-III-R, the author begins with the assessment and then offers descriptions of diagnostic techniques, tools, and rating scales available. The appendices of the book are a number of assessment instruments such as the Dementia Questionnaire, the Mental Status Examination, the Blessed Dementia Rating Scale, etc.

# 13

# *Work and Retirement*

WR1    Abel, B., Hayslip, B. (1987). Locus of control and preparation for retirement. Journal of Gerontology, 42, 162-165.
       Explored the impact of retirement and retirement preparation on perceptions of personal control. Retirement was associated with a shift toward externality, and retirement preparation had but a temporary impact of perceptions of control.

WR2    American Association of Retired Persons (1988). How to train older workers. Washington, DC.
       Well presented discussion of the many problems older workers face as well as strategies that both employees and employers can use to overcome career burnout, career plateauing and career obsolescence.

WR3    American Association of Retired Persons (1989). Business and older workers: Current perceptions and new directions for the 1990's. Washington, DC.
       Discusses the basis for attitudes toward older workers in the business world and the results of a study of management's attitudes toward older workers.

WR4    Antonosky, A., & Sagy, S. (1990). Confronting developmental tasks in the retirement transition. The Gerontologist, 30, 362-368.
       This thought provoking paper takes an Eriksonian perspective in evaluating the impact and meaning of retirement for older adults.

WR5    Atchley, R. M. (1988). Employment and retirement. In R. M.
       Atchley (Ed.), Social forces and aging (pp. 178-205). Belmont, CA:
       Wadsworth.
           Excellent discussion of the employment problems of older workers,
       the retirement process and the impact of retirement.

WR6    Bosse, R., Aldwin, C. M., Levenson, M. R., & Ekerdt, D. (1987).
       Mental health differences between retirees and workers: Findings from
       the normative aging study. Psychology and Aging, 2, 383-389.
           Examined the impact that retirement has on physical and mental
       health in a sample of over 1500 older men. Results suggested retirees
       to report more psychological symptoms than workers controlling for
       physical health. In addition, both early and late retirees reported the
       most psychological symptoms, with late workers reporting the least.

WR7    Bosse, R., Aldwin, C. M., Levenson, M. R., Spiro, A., & Mroczek,
       D. K. (1993). Change in social support after retirement: Longitudinal
       findings from the normative aging study. Journal of Gerontology:
       Psychological Sciences, 48, P210-P217.
           In a longitudinal study of over 1300 men, these authors rejected the
       hypothesis that social support and/or co-worker friendship declines after
       retirement. These findings support the importance of maintaining one's
       convoy of social support throughout adulthood.

WR8    Burrus-Bammel, L. L., & Bammel, G. (1985). Leisure and recreation.
       In J. E. Birren & K. W. Schaie (Eds.), Handbook of the psychology
       of aging (pp. 848-863). New York: Van Nostrand Reinhold.
           Dated, but valuable discussion of the meaning of leisure and its role
       in influencing adjustment among elderly persons.

WR9    Commonwealth Fund (1993). The untapped resource: A final report
       of the Americans over 55 at work program. New York: The Common-
       wealth Fund.
           Executive summary of a series of studies exploring questions of the
       extent to which persons over 55 desire to work longer as well as to
       identify workplace changes to allow this to occur. Excellent resource.

WR10   Cutler, S. J., & Hendricks, J. (1990). Leisure and time use across the
       life course. In R. H. Binstock & L. George (Eds.), Handbook of aging
       and the social sciences (pp. 169-185). New York: Academic Press.
           This comprehensive source discusses conceptual and research issues
       as they apply to leisure and the frequency of leisure behaviors in
       adulthood. Examines the future of leisure in light of changing
       demographics, government intervention, and economic constraints.

WR11   Czaja, S. J., & Glascock, A. P. (1994). Special issue: Cognition, work, technology, and environmental design for the elderly. Experimental Aging Research, 20, 245-311.

A series of articles dealing with the interface of work, cognition and environmental design. Specific contributions deal with cognition-work relationships, career development, technology at home, product development for the aged consumer, and falls.

WR12   Ekerdt, D. J. (1989). Retirement preparation. Annual Review of Gerontology and Geriatrics, 9, 321-356.

Excellent review of the literature pertaining to retirement preparation programs and both their use and efficacy in the business world.

WR13   Ekerdt, D. J., Bosse, R., & Levkoff, S. (1985). An empirical test for phases of retirement: Findings from the Normative Aging Study. Journal of Gerontology, 40, 95-101.

This study presents data suggesting that retirement adjustment is a gradual process through which men proceed. Each phase is characterized by different orientations toward work and retirement.

WR14   Ekerdt, D. J., Vinick, B. H., & Bosse, R. (1989). Orderly endings: Do men know when they will retire? Journal of Gerontology: Social Sciences, 44, 528-535,

This longitudinal study examines the orderliness of retirement from a subjective pre-retirement perspective, finding evidence for both orderly, predictable retirement as well as unplanned, unpredictable withdrawal from the work force.

WR15   Floyd, F., Haynes, S., Rogers-Doll, E., Winemiller, D., Lemsky, C., Burgy, T. M., Werle, M., & Heilman, N. (1992). Assessing retirement satisfaction and retirement experiences. Psychology and Aging, 7, 609-621.

Reports on the development of a measure of retirement as a life transition. Evidence regarding its factor structure, reliability and validity is presented.

WR16   Glamser, F. D., & Hayslip, B. (1985). The impact of retirement on participation in leisure activities. Therapeutic Recreation Journal, 19, 28-38.

Differentiated numerous leisure activities in a longitudinal study, finding overall declines in activity, great between-person variability and a clear pattern of nonparticipation.

WR17    Havighurst, R. J. (1982). The world of work. In J. Wolman (Ed.), Handbook of developmental psychology (pp. 771-787). Englewood Cliffs, NJ: Prentice Hall.
        Well presented chapter on diverse career paths for men and women as well as a traditional discussion of occupational developmental tasks in late life. Traditional orientation toward work, retirement, yet it is historically important.

WR18    Higginbottom, S. F., Barling, J., & Kelloway, E. K. (1993). Linking retirement experiences and marital satisfaction: A mediational model. Psychology and Aging, 8, 508-516.
        Reports on the development of a causal model examining the quality of retirement as an influence on marital satisfaction in later life. Alternative models are proposed and evaluated as well.

WR19    Kelly, J. R., Steinkamp, M., & Kelly, J. (1986). Later-life leisure: How they play in Peoria. The Gerontologist, 26, 531-537.
        Found both consistency and differences in leisure activities with age. Dependent upon the active/passive and family/other distinctions, age effects were nil. With age, travel, cultural and social activities became more important, with family activities predominanting for the oldest age group.

WR20    McFarland, P. A. (1973). The need for functional age measurements in industrial gerontology. Industrial Gerontology, 1, 1-19.
        Advocates the use of functional age in lieu of chronological age as a barameter of skills and performance. Pivotal article in the aging and work literature.

WR21    McGuire, F. A., Dottavio, D., & O'Leary, J. T. (1986). Constraints to participation in outdoor recreation across the life span: A nationwide study of limitors and prohibitors. The Gerontologist, 26, 538-544.
        Distinguishes between limiting and prohibiting factors in outdoor recreational activities. For older adults, lack of money as well as the lack of a partner were important in contraining or prohibiting leisure activity.

WR22    Miletich, J. J. (1986). Retirement: An annotated bibliography. Westport, CT: Greenwood Press.
        Comprehensive bibliographic resource focusing on distinct aspects of the experience of retirement. Includes specific chapters on retirement planning, adjustment to retirement, crime, housing, women and retirement as well as the relationship of work to retirement.

WR23    Palmore, E. B., Burchette, B. M., Fillenbaum, G. C., George, L. K., & Wallman, L. M. (1985). Retirement: Causes and consequences. New York: Springer.
        Comprehensive, though somewhat dated examination of the process of retirement utilizing a variety of databases. While very technical, it contains valuable information on the predictors and consequences of retirement, as well as that pertaining to why persons retire, the role of work in retirement, and factors influencing adjustment to retirement. Includes several chapters on racial, gender and socioeconomic aspects of retirement.

WR24    Parnes, H. S., Crowley, J. E., Haurin, R. J., Less, L. J., Morgan, W. R., Mott, F. L., & Nestel, G. (1985). Retirement among American men. Lexington, MA: Lexington Books.
        Far-reaching broad-based study of the reasons for and the impact of retirement on older men. Rich source of data.

WR25    Quinn, J. F., & Burkhauser, R. V. (1990). Work and retirement. Handbook of aging and the social sciences (pp. 308-327). New York: Academic Press.
        Examines work and retirement, focusing on the retirement decision from an economic perspective. Distinguishes between the impact of involuntary vs. voluntary retirement, as well as a number of very different patterns of withdrawal from the labor force. Excellent, "big picture" treatment of work and retirement for those whose knowledge of economics is limited.

WR26    Robinson, P. K., Coberly, S., & Paul, C. E. (1985). Work and retirement. In R. Binstock & E. Shanas (Eds.), Handbook of aging and the social sciences (pp. 503-527). New York: Van Nostrand Reinhold.
        Excellent, though somewhat dated, discussion of issues of work and retirement at both the individual, employer, and societal levels.

WR27    Sterns, H. L., & Alexander, R. A. (1987). Industrial gerontology: The aging individual and work. In K. W. Schaie (Ed.), Annual review of gerontology and geriatrics: V. 7 (pp. 243-264). New York: Springer. (pp. 243-264).
        Examines issues, theory and research relating to industrial gerontology. Though dated, a solid treatment of the field.

WR28    Swein, G. E., Dame, A., & Carmelli, D. (1991). Involuntary retirement, Type A behavior, and current functiong in elderly men: A

27-year follow-up of the Western Collaborative Group Study.
Psychology and Aging, 6, 384-391.

In a study of over 1000 men, Type A men were more likely to see
their retirement as involuntary. Those whose retirement was involuntary were in poorer health, had poorer adjustment to retirement, and
showed more depressive symptoms, regardless of whether they were
Type A or not.

WR29   Welford, A. T. (1993). Work capacity across the adult years. In R.
Kastenbaum (Ed.), Encyclopedia of adult development (pp. 541-553).
Phoenix, AZ: Oryx Press.

Excellent, though somewhat brief discussion of the effects of age on
a variety of indicators of work performance. Very well written;
presents some unique data.

# 14

# *Death and Dying*

D1      Aiken, L. R. (1991). <u>Dying, death, and bereavement</u>. Boston: Allyn & Bacon.

This book surveys the topic of death and dying in an interdisciplinary manner. It is complete enough to serve as the principal text in a semester course on death and dying but brief enough to be used as a supplementary text in many other courses. This second edition includes information on new topics such as moral issues and court cases concerned with abortion and euthanasia, the problem of AIDS and other deadly diseases, the growth of health psychology and behavioral medicine, and the increased social and political concerns for health care of the elderly.

D2      Cook, A. S., & Oltjenbruns, K. A. (1989). <u>Dying and grieving: Lifespan and family perspective</u>. New York: Holt, Reinhart, and Winston.

Very readable text discussion of death-related issues from a lifespan perspective. Excellent coverage of family bereavement, as well as developmental (child, adolescent, adult) topics. Concluding chapter on caregiving is timely. Suitable for undergraduate courses.

D3      Corr, C. A., Nabe, C. M., & Corr, D. M. (1994). <u>Death and dying, living and life</u>. Pacific Grove, CA: Brooks/Cole.

This text is appropriate for undergraduates and graduate students. It offers information on death, dying, bereavement, life cycle perspectives on death, legal, conceptual, and moral issues of death, and also discusses AIDS as the new death related challenge.

D4      Crenshaw, D. A. (1990). Bereavement: Counseling the grieving throughout the life cycle. New York: Continuum.
        The author provides practical suggestions for helping readers to understand the grief of others. He provides an understanding of the seven tasks of mourning, and discusses the consequences of unresolved grief and the importance of social contacts. There are case examples throughout the book which illustrate bereavement and constructive interventions when dealing with people of all ages. One chapter is entitled "Helping the elderly to grieve."

D5      DeVries, B., Bluck, S., & Birren, J.E. (1993). The understanding of death and dying in a life span perspective. The Gerontologist, 33, 366-372.
        Based on rated content of essays from adults of varying ages, the salience of death exceeded that of dying, and individuals seemed to involve others in a more simplistic manner. While dying was most emphasized in the middle aged, death and dying were generally regarded as very impactful and difficult to accept.

D6      Crisis, Special Issue: Suicide in the Elderly, V. 12, 1991.
        This issue of Crisis focuses solely on the critical issue of elderly suicide. Articles included target theoretical as well as practical issues.

D7      DeSpelder, L. A., & Strickland, A. L. (1992). The last dance: Encountering death and dying (3rd ed.). Palo Alto, CA: Mayfield Publishing.
        Very readable, down-to-earth presentation of a variety of death-related topic. Specialized chapters on cultural variations in death, medical ethics, legal aspects of death, and funerals. Breadth of coverage is excellent. Book is well-received by undergraduates.

D8      Dickenson, D., & Johnson, M. (Eds.). (1993). Death, dying, and bereavement. London: Sage.
        This book provides a variety of writings on the area of death and dying from personal accounts to statistical reports. It presents both sides to some controversial topics such as assisted death. The book does not include a great deal on elderly adults.

D9      Farberow, N.L., Gallagher-Thompson, D., Gilewski, M., & Thompson, L. (1992). Changes in grief and mental health of bereaved spouses of older suicides. Journal of Gerontology: Psychological Sciences, 47, P357-P366.
        This study focused on the difficult adjustments older spouses must make after the suicide of their mates. For at least one year, relative to

those whose spouses have died naturally, survivors report greater depression and less mental health. Even after 2 1/2 years, feelings of sadness and loss persist for both groups despite improved overall functioning.

D10    Gabriel, R. M., & Kirshling, J. M. (1989). Assessing grief among the bereaved elderly: A review of existing measures. Hospice Journal, 5, 29-54.
    This review reviews the nine most widely cited measures used to assess the bereaved elderly. The authors provide a rating instrument for use in comparing potential measures while describing each measure and its reliability and validity.

D11    Gilmore, A., & Gilmore, S. (1988). A safer death: Multidisciplinary aspects of terminal care. New York: Plenum.
    This volume contains papers presented at the International Conference on Multidisciplinary Aspects of Terminal care organized by The Prince and Princess of Wales Hospice in Glasgow, Scotland, U.K. The contributors come from a variety of perspectives (e.g. sociological, psychoanalytic, psycho-existential) and address different populations (e.g. children, elderly, nurses). The multicultural and multidisciplinary nature of the works included provides valuable information for any interested reader.

D12    Hansson, R. O., Stroebe, M. S., & Stroebe, W. (1988). Bereavement and widowhood. Journal of Social Issues, 44.
    The whole issue is devoted to state of the art contributions to the topics of "Theories of Grief, Mourning, and Bereavement," "Symptomatology and Outcomes of Bereavement," and "Coping, Counseling, and Therapy." First-rate contributors. One of the best possible sources for information and informed discussion on bereavement research and therapy. Several articles deal specifically with elderly people.

D13    Harper, B. C. (1989). Serving the dying client. In R. H. Hull, & K. M. Griffin (Eds.), Communication disorders in aging (pp. 131-140). Newbury Park, CA: Sage.
    This chapter discusses important issues to be considered when counseling a dying client including one's own mortality, communicating with dying persons, and the Dying Person's Bill of Rights. Anxiety, adaptation, coping behaviors and denial are other topics discussed.

D14    Hayslip, B., & Leon, J. (1992). Hospice care. Newbury Park, CA: Sage Publishers.

An overview of the development of the hospice movement as well as specific chapters on organizational and policy-related aspects of hospice, the interdisciplinary team, work with patients and families and grief and bereavement.

D15    Kalish, R. A. (1985). The social context of death and dying. In R. Binstock & E. Shanas (Eds.), Handbook of aging and the social sciences (pp. 149-172). New York: Van Nostrand Reinhold.
       Well-written though somewhat dated discussion of the impact of the cultural values about death and dying on older adults.

D16    Kalish, R.A. (1987). Death and dying. In P. Silverman (Ed.), The elderly as modern pioneers (pp. 389-405). Bloomington, IN: Indiana Univ. Press.
       This chapter offers discussion on the meaning of death, aging and being elderly, death, dying and the dead, grief, mourning and bereavement, and the process of dying and bereavement.

D17    Kastenbaum, R. (1992). Psychology of death. New York: Springer.
       This section edition reflects changes in attitudes toward death as well as the birth of alternatives to institutional dying as well as an awareness of the problems of technology for defining death. Chapters reflect the author's most intense interests. For example, they deal with deathbed scenes, as world without death, as well as several excellent chapters on the developmental aspects of death.

D18    Kearl, M. C. (1989). Endings: A sociology of death and dying. New York: Oxford University Press.
       An extremely sensitive, artfully written book dealing with topics not usually found in most sources, e.g., death and work, the politics of dying, death and the military experience, religion and death. This text would serve as an excellent complement to those whose focus is more psychological. Suitable for both graduate and undergraduate courses.

D19    Kirsling, R. A. (1986). Review of suicide among elderly persons. Psychological Reports, 59, 359-366.
       Reviews the literature on suicide among elderly persons. Incidence rates from the US and other countries are discussed, and suicide rates are noted for the general population and by specific age and sex subgroups. Factors contributing to elderly suicide and possible preventive strategies are also discussed.

D20    Leenaars, A. A. (1991). Life span perspectives on suicide: Time-lines in the suicide process. New York: Plenum.

This book has been conceptualized based on the recent shift to viewing suicide across the life from a developmental perspective. The authors hope that understanding the time-lines in the suicidal process can assist in preventing suicide, from childhood through adulthood to old age.

D21    Levy, S. M. (1990). Humanizing death: Psychotherapy with terminally ill patients. In P. Costa & G. Vandenbos (Eds.), <u>Psychological aspects of serious illness: Chronic conditions, fatal diseases, and clinical care</u> (pp. 185-213). Washington, DC: American Psychological Association.
        Sensitively written chapter on a topic rarely addressed. Ethics of terminal care, the needs of dying patients and their families, hospice, interventions with dying persons as well as research issues are discussed.

D22    Logue, B. J. (1993). <u>Death control and the elderly in America</u>. New York: Lexington Books/Macmillan.
        In this book, the author reviews the medical, social, ethical, and legal issues associated with death and dying and puts current problems in historical and cross-cultural perspective. She incorporates studies from a variety of disciplines, including gerontology, sociology, psychology, medicine, and bioethics, to explain why death control is necessary, why it may be advantageous, and why it may be hazardous.

D23    Lund, D. (1989). <u>Older bereaved spouses</u>. New York: Hemisphere.
        This edited volume contains a series of excellent empirically based chapters by the author as well as other prominent bereavement researchers exploring the impact and course of bereavement, factors influencing bereavement adjustment, and comparisons between bereavement and divorce. Concluding chapter integrates those preceeding it.

D24    Margolis, O. S., Kutscher, A. H., Marcus, E. R., Raether, H. C. Pine, V. R., Seeland, I. B., & Cherico, D. J. (1988). <u>Grief and the loss of an adult child</u>. New York: Praeger.
        The essays included in this book are written by scholars, clinicians, social workers, and individuals who have experience the loss of an adult child in their personal lives. The proposed philosophy of caregiving is one that reinforces alternative ways of enhancing the quality of life, introduces interventions based on the emotional well-being of all involved, and fosters more mature understandings of the dying process, problems of separation, loss, bereavement, and grief.

D25     Marshall, V. W., & Levy, J. A. (1990). Aging and dying. Handbook
        of aging and the social sciences (pp. 245-262). New York: Academic
        Press.
            Discusses death and dying in later life at both the societal and
        individual levels. Focuses on the dying process in terms of its impact
        on the older adult and both family and non-family caregivers, the
        community and society in general.

D26     McIntosh, J. L., Santos, J. F., Hubbard, R. W., & Overholser, J. C.
        (1994). Elder suicide: Research, theory, and treatment. Washington,
        DC: American Psychological Association.
            Comprehensive resource dealing with the incidence, dynamics and
        treatment of older adults who have attempted and/or completed suicide.
        Specific discussion of risk factors, ethics and assessment.

D27     Moss, M. S., & Moss, S. Z. (1989). Death of the very old. In K. J.
        Doka (Ed.), Disenfranchised grief (pp. 213-227). Lexington, MA:
        Lexington Books/D.C. Heath and Company.
            This chapter discusses deaths of elderly persons in the United States
        and examines the bereavement in response to the death of very old
        persons (aged eighty or over). The authors suggest that when the
        survivor and the deceased are both very old, the grief is doubly
        disenfranchised partly due to societal devaluation of the very old.
        Older person's death attitudes and the social context of the death of
        older persons are also discussed.

D28     Norris, F. H., & Murrell, S. A. (1987). Older adult family stress and
        adaptation before and after bereavement. Journal of Gerontology, 42,
        606-612.
            The findings presented in this article are based on data collected
        from pre- and postinterviews with 63 older adults who had experienced
        the death of a spouse, parent, or child and with 387 older adults who
        had not been bereaved. The relationships between family stress,
        health, and psychological distress are discussed in terms of how they
        relate to bereavement.

D29     Osgood, N. J., Brant, B. A., & Lipman, A. (1991). Suicide among the
        elderly in long-term care facilities. Westport, CT: Greenwood.
            This book describes the unique aspects of the elderly experience of
        institutionalized living and discusses the possible relationship between
        such living and suicide.

D30     Osgood, N. J., & Thielman, S. (1990). Geriatric suicidal behavior:
        Assessment and treatment. In S. J. Blumenthal, & D. J. Kupfer (Eds.),

Suicide over the life cycle (pp. 341-379). Washington, D.C.: American Psychiatric Press.

This chapter discusses some of the distinctions between suicide in the young and old, with the old being less likely to communicate their intentions, more likely to use lethal methods, and less likely to attempt as a means of gaining attention. Assessment and treatment issues are also discussed.

D31      Osterweis, M. (1985). Bereavement and the elderly. Aging, 348, 8-13, 41.

The information presented in this article is drawn from a large report on bereavement by M. Osterweis et al. (1984). The author discusses the process of bereavement among the elderly and suggests that in this process a person's emotional, social, and physiological functioning may be altered for more than a year. She also discusses the special problems which may confront older adults such as previous ill health, lack of social support, and lack of resources.

D32      Parkes, C. M. (1988). Research: Bereavement. Omega, 18, 365-378.

A review article detailing bereavement and its effects on humans by one of the pioneers in the field. The breadth of coverage and clarity of writing set this article apart from others. Part of a special issue of Omega dealing with research in Thanatology.

D33      Richman, J. (1993). Preventing elderly suicide: Overcoming personal despair, professional neglect, and social bias. New York: Springer.

This book explores some of the major social, biological, situational, and psychological conditions associated with elderly suicide, how to recognize the strengths and assets of the elderly, as well as the foundations of theory, assessment, and practice of the therapist. The authors primary focus is upon the treatment and prevention of direct suicidal reactions and he presents the psychotherapeutic procedures he has found most effective in practice.

D34      Sanders, C. M. (1989). Grief: The mourning after. New York: John Wiley & Sons.

Adult bereavement is the focus. A useful summary of bereavement theory is followed by research-based discussions of "Phases of Bereavement," "Moderator Variables," and "Types of Bereavement," concluding with recommendations for "Interventions with the Bereaved." The "Moderator Variables" section is distinctive and especially valuable. As a grieving person who became a significant researcher and clinician, the author knows her subject well. Mostly for professionals, but also suitable for college students and educated adults.

D35    Stillion, J. M, McDowell, E. E., & May, J. H. (1989). <u>Suicide across the life span</u>. New York: Hemisphere.
       This is a book designed as an introduction to the complex issue of suicide for advanced undergraduates or beginning graduate students. The authors synthesize available information and also report their original research done to supplement fragmented or outdated knowledge. The focus of the book is on the interaction between developing individuals and their environments through development. One chapter is focused on suicide among elderly persons.

D36    Stroebe, M. S., Stroebe, W., & Hannson, R. O. (Eds.). (1993). <u>Handbook of bereavement: Theory, research, and intervention</u>. New York: Cambridge University Press.
       This excellent volume provides bereavement research from a wide variety of theoretical orientations. The topics covered in the text include the phenomenology and measurement of grief, current theories of grief, and the physiological, psychological, and social impacts of bereavement. Different grief reactions to bereavement and important counseling issues are also discussed.

D37    Valente, S. M. (1993-94). Suicide and elderly people: Assessment and intervention. <u>Omega</u>, <u>28</u>, 317-331.
       The author provides a case study and then discusses the risk assessment and interventions used. A practical approach to early detection, evaluation, and management of suicide risk is presented. A table is included which lists the criteria for the assessment of rational suicide.

D38    Wass, H., Berardo, F., & Neimeyer, R. (1989). <u>Dying: Facing the facts</u>. New York: McGraw-Hill.
       This edited volume contains well-referenced chapters on a variety of aspects of death and dying to include for example, grief and bereavement, death anxiety, and funerals.

D39    Wilkinson-Tjoa, D. (1989). Loss, death, and living. In E. S. Deichman, & R. Kociecki (Eds.), <u>Working with the elderly: An introduction</u> (pp. 275-295). Buffalo, NY: Prometheus.
       This chapter touches on many of the important loss issues of the elderly. Included topics are the loss of one's own life, maturational losses, situational losses, and identity losses. The process of grief and effective grieving are discussed. The author also suggests ways to help in the healing and dying processes.

D40 Williamson, J. B., & Schneidman, E. S. (1995). <u>Death: Current perspectives (4th ed)</u>. Mountain View, CA: Mayfield.

Recently revised interdisciplinary text contains selected chapters covering the psycholosical and ethical aspects of death and dying. Specific discussions of euthanasia, medical ethics, funerals, culture and death, and AIDS are included. This edited volume would be an excellent complement to other authored texts as it contains both classic and more contemporary works in the field.

D41 Wisocki, P. A., & Averill, J. R. (1987). The challenge of bereavement. In L. L. Carstensen, & B. A. Edelstein (Eds.), <u>Handbook of clinical gerontology</u> (pp. 312-321). Elmsford, NY: Pergamon.

This chapter briefly reviews the sequelae of bereavement among the elderly and outlines the relevant clinical issues for assisting bereaved older adults. Grief reactions, normal grief, and the relationship between bereavement and health are also discussed.

D42 Worden, J. W. (1991). <u>Grief counseling and grief therapy: A handbook for the health practitioner</u>. New York: Springer.

The author details the mechanisms of normal grief and the procedures for helping clients accomplish the "tasks of mourning." He goes on to explain how unresolved grief can lead to problems requiring psychotherapy, and how the therapist can diagnose and treat problems related to exaggerated, chronic, masked, and delayed grief reactions. Worden includes a section on grief and the elderly.

# Author Index

# Subject Index

**About the Compilers**

BERT HAYSLIP, JR. is Regents Professor of Psychology at the University of North Texas and is Chair of the Doctoral Program in Experimental Psychology. He has published over 80 articles and book chapters on a variety of topics in psychogerontology and thanatology in such outlets as *The Journal of Gerontology*, *Psychology and Aging*, *Experimental Aging Research*, *The Gerontologist*, *Omega: Journal of Death and Dying*, and *The International Journal of Aging and Human Development*. He currently serves as associate editor of *Experimental Aging Research*. He is senior author of *Adult Development and Aging* (2nd ed., 1993) and *Hospice Care* (1992). He is a fellow of the Gerontological Society of America and the American Psychological Association. His research interests include intellectual functioning and aging, caregiving, death anxiety, hospice care, grief and bereavement, personality and aging, and mental health and aging.

HEATHER L. SERVATY is a doctoral candidate in Counseling Psychology at the University of North Texas. Her interests are in aging, death and dying, as well as life span development.

AMIE S. WARD is a doctoral candidate in Experimental Psychology at the University of North Texas. Her interests are in the psychophysiology of drug use and drug addiction, and cognition and aging.